THE
GOOD COOK'S
COMPANION

THE
GOOD COOK'S
COMPANION

by Audrey Senturia and Ruth Ann Rubin
Illustrations by Patrick Blackwell

A
YANKEE
MAGAZINE
PUBLICATION

Published 1981 by
YANKEE, Inc.
Dublin, New Hampshire 03444

First Edition
Second Printing, 1981
Copyright 1981, by Yankee, Inc.
Printed in the United States of America

Library of Congress Catalog Card No. 80-85482
ISBN 0-911658-27-0

CONTENTS

Standard Sizes   69

Substitutions   73

This Makes That   75

Kitchen Tips   79

AUTHORS' FOREWORD

I n this basic culinary dictionary, we have com-
piled cooking terms and foods most commonly
used in recipes or found in cookbooks or
restaurant menus. The choice of terms was based
on usage. Foreign terms included are those that have
crept into the American language of gastronomy and
are now in general use. All of the approximately 1200
definitions are listed alphabetically. The text also
includes brief sections on: 1) Baking Times & Temperatures; 2) Measures & Measurements; 3) Oversize
Wine Bottles; 4) Servings & Pounds; 5) Standard
Sizes; 6) Substitutions; 7) This Makes That; and 8)
Kitchen Tips.

We hope the magic appeal of words and their
meanings will add to your joy of cooking and
enhance your culinary experiences.

— *Audrey Senturia and Ruth Ann Rubin*

A CULINARY DICTIONARY

Abalone: A large mollusk with a clam-like flavor.

Absinthe (Fr.): A liqueur made from wormwood leaves that have been macerated and distilled, and flavored with other aromatic plants, such as fennel, hyssop, or Chinese anise.

Absorbent Paper: Any paper that will absorb liquid or fat easily. Newspaper, brown bag or wrapping paper, and paper towels are all excellent absorbent papers.

Acacia: The blossoms of the acacia tree, sprinkled with sugar and steeped in rum, are used for making dessert fritters. Infused in white alcohol and sugar, the blossoms make a homemade ratafia, or liqueur.

Acetic Acid: This is the basis of vinegar (q.v.); used in candy-making.

Acidulated Water: Water with vinegar or lemon juice added. The term is also used to describe carbonated mineral water.

Acorn: Fruit of the oak tree. Some types are eaten raw or roasted. Ground roasted acorns from the Spanish ballota oak are used as a coffee substitute.

Adjust: A term used in relation to seasonings meaning that one should taste the dish before serving and add seasonings as required.

Adobo (Sp.): A Mexican sauce made with vinegar, chilies, and other seasonings.

After-Dinner Coffee: Strong black coffee served after dinner in demitasses (q.v.).

Agar-Agar: A thickening agent with a neutral taste obtained from seaweed. Thin strips are dissolved in boiling water to make a stiff jelly.

Agave: A Mexican cactus whose fermented pulp is used to make an alcoholic beverage called "pulque" (q.v.).

Aiguillette (Fr.): Thin slice cut lengthwise from the breast of poultry or winged game.

Aïoli (Ital.): A mayonnaise sauce strongly flavored with garlic.

Aji Oil: An Oriental oil flavored with sesame seeds, chilies, or cayenne.

À la, à l', au (Fr.): In the manner of.

Albacore: A species of tuna or tunny fish (q.v.). Also, the Portuguese name for swordfish.

Al Dente (Ital.): A term describing food, especially pasta, but also vegetables, cooked so they are still slightly firm to the bite.

Allemande Sauce: A white sauce made from meat, chicken, or fish stock and enriched with egg yolks and cream.

Alligator Pear: An avocado.

Allspice: An aromatic spice made from the berry of the *Eugenia pimento* tree, found in the West Indies. Used whole or ground, it tastes like a combination of nutmeg, cloves, and cinnamon, hence the name. Used in pickling, fruitcakes, and other dessert dishes, and with certain meats.

Allumettes (Fr.): Literally, "little matchsticks," but, in cooking, actually strips or cakes of puff pastry enclosing various mixtures. Used as hot hors d'oeuvres.

Almond: Nut fruit of the almond tree. Almond trees, depending on their variety, can produce either sweet or bitter almond nuts. Both are used in cooking. (The oil of bitter almonds is poisonous.)

Almond Paste: A prepared mixture used to make macaroons (q.v.) and other sweet treats; made of sugar, ground almonds, and dried eggs.

Almond Sauce: Usually consists of crushed sweet almonds combined with bread crumbs; used with fish, chicken, or turkey.

Amandine (Fr.): Describes any dish or sauce prepared with sautéed sweet almonds.

Amaretti (Ital.): Macaroons (q.v.). Amaretto is a liqueur.

Ambrosia: Refers to a dessert or fruit salad, usually consisting of oranges, coconut, and marshmallows.

Amontillado (Sp.): A dry sherry of Spain.

Ananas (Fr.): Pineapple.

Anchovy: A small sea fish usually found tinned in olive oil or brine.

Anchovy Sauce: Fresh or salted anchovies in a basic roux or sauce with wine added for flavoring.

Ancienne, à l' (Fr.): Sauces and garnishes prepared in the "old-time" way.

Angelica: Large perennial herb used to flavor various liqueurs; it is also candied, used in baking, or eaten plain.

Angels on Horseback: A hot hors d'oeuvre prepared by wrapping fresh oysters each in a thin slice of bacon and then broiling them.

Anglaise, à l' (Fr.): "English-style;" describes meats, poultry, or vegetables cooked in water, or fish poached in a simple court-bouillon (q.v.).

Angostura: The bark of a Venezuelan plant of the rue family used to flavor bitters.

Aniseed: The seed of the anise plant used to give a licorice-like flavor to coleslaw, sauerkraut, creamed cabbage or cauliflower, beets, cookies, and cakes.

Anisette: French liqueur made from aniseed.

Antipasto (Ital.): Italian assortment of appetizers.

Apéritif (Fr.): A drink, usually alcoholic, served before a meal and believed to stimulate the appetite. The term can apply to anything from vermouth to scotch whiskey.

À Point (Fr.): Not overcooked, not undercooked, just right.

Appenzeller (Ger.): One of the three great Swiss cheeses with holes. Has a nutty flavor and a rather strong odor.

Appetizers: Attractive small open-faced sandwiches or small portions of foods or beverages served before a meal or as a first course; also served at cocktail parties.

Aquavit: A clear liquor flavored with caraway seed; popular in Scandinavian countries.

Arlésienne, à l' (Fr.): Name given to certain vegetable garnishes, including tomatoes.

Armagnac: A region in the French province of Gascony that is famous for the brandy bearing its name.

Aromatics: Vegetables, fine herbs, or other ingredients such as seaweed that are steamed with meat and fish to impart both flavor and aroma.

Arrowroot: A very fine flour used as a thickening agent.

10

Asafetida: Gum resin from an Oriental palm; used in Asian cooking.

Asiago (Ital.): A hard Italian cheese excellent for grating.

Aspic: A clear jelly usually made from meat or fish stock and used to coat fish, vegetables, or fruit. Also applied to the opaque red jelly made from tomato juice stiffened with gelatin.

Aubergine (Fr.): Eggplant.

Aurore Sauce: A velouté sauce (q.v.) with tomato puree added. Used for eggs, sweetbreads, or fowl.

Avgelemono Soup: Greek soup made of lamb or chicken broth, rice, eggs, and lemon.

Baba (Russ.): Cake made of leavened dough mixed with raisins and steeped in kirsch or rum after cooking.

Bacardi: A well-known Cuban rum.

Bagel: A variety of roll made of yeast dough formed into a small doughnut-like shape, cooked in simmering water, and then baked in the oven.

Bain Marie (Fr.): A French cooking utensil consisting of a bath of heated water in which pans are set to keep food warm without further cooking. Similar to the double boiler (q.v.) in principle.

Bake: To cook by dry heat, usually in an oven. When applied to meats and poultry, the process is called roasting.

Baked Alaska: A dessert made of cakes (usually sponge cake), topped with very firm ice cream, then completely covered with a meringue (q.v.) and baked in a hot oven until the meringue is lightly browned.

Baking Powder: A combination of several chemical ingredients used to increase the size of dough and lighten its texture; usually contains cream of tartar and sodium bicarbonate.

Baklava (Gr.): A rich honey-nut confection made with filo (phyllo) dough (q.v.).

Ballottine (Fr.): A kind of galantine (q.v.) served as a hot or cold entrée and usually made of a piece of meat, fowl, game, or fish that is boned and rolled into a round "balloon-like" bundle.

Bamboo Shoots: The tender, spiky tips of young bamboo plants, which, eaten raw or pickled, have a delicate, nut-like flavor.

Bangers: Slang term used in England for sausages, particularly the fat, cereal-stuffed breakfast sausages.

Bannock: A flat, Scottish cake made of barley or oatmeal.

Barbecue Sauce: An American sauce that can be purchased bottled or made at home in many versions (most containing chili and Worcestershire sauce, vinegar, and tomatoes); it is brushed on meats or poultry during grilling.

Barberry: A common prickly shrub with a berry that can be pickled green, like capers (q.v.), or made into a meat jelly when red-ripe.

Bard: To cover breasts of birds with thin slices of bacon or salt pork to keep them moist without basting while roasting.

Bar-le-Duc (Fr.): A French fruit preserve made of currants or gooseberries.

Baron: Of beef — twin sirloins cooked together; of lamb — the hindquarters, including both legs and loins.

Barquette (Fr.): A small, boat-shaped pastry shell.

Baste: To moisten meat or other food while roasting or baking with juices spooned up from the pan or with added liquids.

Bâtarde Sauce (Fr.): A butter sauce

11

(butter, flour, water, and egg yolk) used for vegetables or boiled fish.

Batter: A semiliquid mixture that may include flour, water, milk, eggs, and butter; a coating for fried food; a cake or pancake mixture.

Batterie de Cuisine (Fr.): Kitchen equipment in general.

Bavarian Cream: A cold, moulded dessert composed of custard, gelatin, and whipped cream.

Bavarian Sauce: Made with wine vinegar, butter, horseradish, and nutmeg; served hot with fish.

Bay Leaves: A traditional ingredient of a bouquet garni (q.v.); also used alone in meat, fish, or poultry dishes, soups, and stews.

Bean Curd: A creamy, firm custard made from soybeans and pressed into squares.

Bean Paste: A salty, fermented sauce prepared from ground yellow soybeans.

Bean Sprouts: Edible sprouts grown from small peas called mung beans.

Bean-Thread Noodle: An opaque, fine, white noodle made from ground mung beans; sometimes referred to as peastarch.

Beard: To remove "beards" of mussels or oysters with a sharp knife.

Béarnaise Sauce: Basically a hollandaise sauce flavored with tarragon, chervil, thyme, and bay leaf. Served with grilled meat or fish.

Beat: To make a mixture smooth with a quick, even motion, using a spoon, wire whisk, or hand or electric beater.

Beater: A utensil that beats, whips, or whisks air into foods.

Beaujolais (Fr.): A favorite red burgundy wine.

Béchamel Sauce: A basic white sauce made from milk, butter, and flour.

Beef Tartare (Fr.): Fresh lean, ground sirloin seasoned with salt, pepper, onions, and capers, in individual servings, each topped with a raw egg. Also served as a spread with crackers,

Melba toast, or other canapé bases.

Beignets (Fr.): Anything dipped in batter and fried in deep fat, such as a fritter.

Bel Paese (Ital.): Medium-soft Italian cheese.

Benedictine: A liqueur invented and still made by the Benedictine monks.

Benzoate of Soda: A widely used food preservative.

Bercy Sauce: Velouté sauce (q.v.) flavored with fish fumet (q.v.), chopped shallots, parsley, white wine, and butter.

Beurre (Fr.): Butter.

Beurre, au (Fr.): Tossed or sautéed in butter.

Beurre Blanc (Fr.): Sauce of white wine, butter, wine vinegar, fish stock, parsley, and chopped shallots. Served with poached or boiled fish, particularly pike.

Beurre Manié (Fr.): Butter kneaded with flour into small balls and added to liquid mixtures as a thickening or binding agent.

Beurre Noir (Fr.): Also known as Brown Butter (although the French term actually means "black butter"), this is clarified melted butter cooked slowly over direct heat to a nut-brown color.

Bien Fatigué (Fr.): Describes a salad of greens tossed with a hot dressing until limp — a wilted-greens salad.

Bigarade (Fr.): Originally a bitter or sour orange, now used to describe foods cooked in orange juice. Bigarade sauce, traditional for duck, is a brown sauce flavored with oranges, and sometimes lemon and curaçao (q.v.).

Bind: To thicken and equalize a mixture so that it does not separate (lentil soup, for example) by adding eggs or melted butter with flour, rice, or potatoes.

Bird's Nest: A semitransparent gelatinous product used in Chinese cookery.

Biscotti (Ital.): Cookies; biscuits.

Bisque: A thick cream soup usually made from fish or seafood; also a rich frozen dessert of ice cream made with crushed macaroons (q.v.).

Black Olives: Olives picked ripe, boiled in brine, then pickled in brine or oil.

Blanc, au (Fr.): Poached or simmered and served with a white sauce.

Blanc Mange (Fr.): A smooth, white, and sweet pudding made with milk and cornstarch and flavored with almonds, vanilla, rum, or brandy.

Blanch: To precook foods in boiling water or steam for a few minutes to prepare them for canning or freezing, or to loosen skin (as of tomatoes) to facilitate peeling.

Blanquette (Fr.): A "white" stew, usually of chicken, lamb, or veal served in a white sauce bound with egg yolks and cream.

Blaze: To pour warmed brandy or liqueur over food and ignite.

Blend: To mix ingredients together until well combined and smooth.

Blender: An electric appliance that whips, chops, mixes, grates, purees, blends, and liquefies.

Bleu, au (Fr.): French term for a method of cooking fish, mainly trout, quickly in boiling court-bouillon (q.v.) or water with vinegar, which imparts a bluish tinge to the skin of the fish so cooked.

Blini (Russ.): Pancakes made with buckwheat flour leavened with yeast. Served with caviar and sour cream or melted butter, or similarly with other fish.

Blintz: A very thin, crêpelike pancake served rolled around various fillings, cottage cheese being one of the most popular.

Bloater: A slightly salted and smoked herring eaten for breakfast in England.

Blue Cheeses: Cheeses incorporating mold. They are similar to Roquefort (q.v.), but less delicate in flavor.

Blue Points: Excellent variety of large oyster.

Bocadillas (Sp.): "Little mouthfuls" — a Mexican word for appetizers.

Boeuf en Daube (Fr.): Beef, usually rump or shoulder, braised in stock and red wine with herbs.

Boil: To cook in water or other liquids kept in continuous motion. The boiling-point temperature at or near sea level is 212° F.

Bok Choy (Chin.): Chinese cabbage (q.v.).

Bolognese Sauce: An Italian sauce of mixed, diced vegetables and tomatoes, flavored with herbs and white wine, and usually served with pasta.

Bombe: Ice cream with a flavored mousse-type center, shaped in a round or conical mould.

Bonbon (Fr.): A small candy, particularly one with icing.

Bone: To remove bones from meat or fowl. A sharp-pointed boning knife is best for this.

Boned and Rolled: Certain meat cuts boned by the butcher and then rolled up and tied for roasting.

Bone Marrow: A soft, fatty, nourishing substance contained in the long hollow bones commonly called marrow bones used in soups. See also Marrow.

Bonito: A fish similar to, but not exactly like, tuna.

Bonne Femme (Fr.): A term used to describe plain, home-style cooking.

Bordelaise Sauce: A brown sauce using red wine for part of the liquid. Served with grilled meats.

Borsch (Russ.): A soup made from beets. Borsch can be either a whole-meal soup, containing a number of other vegetables and meat, or a clear beet broth served with sour cream as an attractive first course.

Bouchée (Fr.): A small patty made of puff pastry (q.v.) that is filled after baking. Literally "a mouthful."

Bouillabaisse (Fr.): A whole-meal soup combining different types of fish and shellfish with vegetables cooked in

13

water and white wine, and flavored with garlic, parsley, saffron, and bay leaf.

Bouillon: A clear, strained soup or stock made from beef, veal, or fowl boiled with vegetables in salted water.

Bouillon Cube: Concentrated, dehydrated form of bouillon (q.v.), reconstituted by adding hot water.

Bouquet Garni (Fr.): A small bunch of fresh or dried herbs tied in cheesecloth and used to flavor stocks and stews; usually made up of parsley, thyme, tarragon, a bay leaf, marjoram, and chervil.

Bouquetière, à la (Fr.): Garnished with a variety of cooked vegetables.

Bourbon: Whiskey distilled from a mash containing no less than 51% corn grain.

Bourguignonne Sauce: Made from chopped shallots, parsley, bay leaves, and mushroom trimmings cooked in red wine, then strained and thickened with beurre manié (q.v.). Served with meats or fish.

Braise: To cook food slowly in a small amount of liquid in a covered pan. The food may or may not be browned first in a small amount of fat.

Brandy: A distilled liquor made from wine or fermented fruit juice.

Brandy Sauce: A hard, brandy-flavored butter sauce served with mince pies or Christmas pudding.

Bread: To coat with bread crumbs before cooking.

Bread Crumbs: Soft bread crumbs, made of fresh white bread, crumbled, are used in cooking, for stuffings, etc. Dry bread crumbs, pulverized with a rolling pin, are used to coat foods before sautéeing or frying.

Bread Sauce: Bread crumbs cooked in milk with shallots or onions, ham, parsley, lemon, and seasonings. In England, traditionally served with roast poultry or game birds.

Brie (Fr.): Brie has been called the greatest of all soft cheeses. It is best eaten when it is runny with or without the rind and white mold.

Brillat-Savarin: A famous French writer on food and a gourmet of high repute.

Brine: A heavily saturated solution of pickling or sea salt in water, used for pickling or as a preservative.

Brioche (Fr.): A cakelike yeast bread, often made in the shape of a circle or a ball surmounted by another, smaller ball. The dough can be used to make cases for sweets or flans and other pastries.

Brochette (Fr.): A spit or skewer used in cooking or broiling.

Broil: To cook over or under direct heat, as in barbecuing or grilling.

Broth: Liquid in which meat, poultry, or vegetables have simmered; same as stock.

Brown: To cook in a little fat at high heat until brown, sealing juices; may be done on top of the stove or in the oven.

Brown Butter: Beurre noir (q.v.).

Brown Butter Sauce: Butter cooked until it bubbles and variously flavored with herbs, capers, and lemon juice or vinegar. Used on eggs, fish, brains, or boiled vegetables.

Brown Sauce: A basic sauce consisting of a browned roux of flour and butter and meat or fish stock.

Brown Sugar: Sugar containing some residue of the molasses in the juice of the sugar cane. The darker brown the sugar, the higher the molasses content.

Bruise: To gently crush the leaves of herbs to release their inner essence.

Brulé, Brulée (Fr.): French word meaning "burnt," used to denote caramelized sugar on a custard dessert, e.g., crème brulée.

Brunoise (Fr.): A mixture of finely diced or shredded vegetables sautéed in butter and used to flavor soups and sauces.

14

Brush: To spread food lightly with salad oil, melted fat, milk, heavy cream, beaten egg, etc., using a pastry brush.

Bucatini (Ital.): Pasta that is hollow like macaroni, but thinner than spaghetti.

Bulgur: Small-grained cracked wheat. There are several different spellings, for example, bulgar, bourghol.

Burdock Root: A long, dark-brown, tapering vegetable root peeled and prepared like salsify.

Burgundy: A region of France famous for its wines; also, generally, the wines of that region.

Burnet: An herb with a cucumberlike flavor, used as an ingredient in many sauces. The leaves are sometimes used in salads.

Burrito (Sp.): A large flour tortilla (q.v.) with a filling.

Butter: A fatty substance extracted from the milk of mammals. Butter can be compounded with other substances to provide innumerable variations, e.g., herb butter, crayfish butter, et al.

Butter Curler: A sharp, serrated metal instrument that, when drawn over the surface of a lump of butter, shaves off a thin curl.

Butterfly: To bone, cut almost in half, and spread flat, as a leg of lamb or loin of pork. The resulting flat slab of meat is usually roasted or grilled.

Buttermilk: Liquid left after butter has been removed from churned cream.

Butter Paddle: A rectangular wooden paddle that is scored on one side and used to make butterballs.

Cacciatore (Ital.): "Hunter's style," denoting meats, poultry, or game cooked in a sauce made with toma-toes, white or red wine, onions, and mushrooms.

Caffé Espresso (Ital.): The strong coffee produced by the Italian method of forcing steam through fine grounds.

Cake Rack or Tray: A slightly elevated, open wire rack on which breads, cakes, or cookies are placed to cool when removed from the oven. The elevation allows the air to circulate under as well as around the baked product.

Calimyrna: A variety of fig.

Calvados (Fr.): French apple brandy from Normandy.

Calzone (Ital.): A macaroni dish pre-pared with cheese and meat.

Camembert (Fr.): One of the great cheeses of France, made in the district of Camembert. It is soft and similar to Brie in texture, but stronger in flavor.

Camomile: A common herb used to make tea and sometimes used to flavor vermouths or other apéritifs.

Canapé (Fr.): A small piece of crustless, fancy-cut toast or sautéed bread, spread with highly seasoned food and garnished. Served with cocktails. See also Hors d'Oeuvres.

Candy: To preserve food, as orange peel, by boiling with sugar, which forms a hard coating. Also a confec-tion.

Cannelloni (Ital.): Rectangles of noodle dough rolled into a tube; usually stuffed with a meat filling, arranged in a dish, and doubly sauced with béchamel and tomato sauces before baking.

Cannoli (Ital.): A dessert consisting of pastry tubes filled with ricotta, choco-late, and candied fruit.

Cap: The cover used to seal a preserving jar. There are three kinds: (1) the two-piece metal cap that consists of a screw band and a lid fitted with a ring of sealing compound; (2) the one-piece zinc cap lined with white porce-lain and used with a rubber ring fitted onto the neck of the jar; and (3) the glass cap, also used with a rubber ring, and sealed with the wire bail attached to the jar.

Capers: The unopened flower buds of the caper plant, preserved in vinegar and used as a condiment.

Caper Sauce: Plain butter, brown, or Hollandaise sauce enhanced with capers; served with salmon, lamb, or white fish.

Capon: A rooster that has been castrated to improve its flesh. Usually weighs more than 5 pounds and is very desirable for roasting.

Caponata (Ital.): A combination of eggplant, capers, black olives, celery, anchovy, onion, tomato puree and vinegar, parsley, and seasonings. Best served cold as an appetizer.

Capellini (Ital.): Translated as "fine hairs;" one of the very thin varieties of flat spaghetti.

Cappelletti (Ital.): The word means "little hats." Pasta dumplings cut in the shape of small, peaked hats and stuffed with meat.

Caramel: Sugar melted and browned or sugar syrup cooked to a deep-brown color; also a type of chewy candy.

Caramelize: To melt granulated sugar over low heat until it changes color to golden brown without scorching or burning, which would impart a bitter taste.

Caraway: A plant producing black seeds that are very pungent and have many culinary uses. Also used to mean the seeds themselves.

Carbonade (Fr.): A beef stew cooked with beer; of Belgian origin.

Cardamom: A plant species of the ginger family, whose aromatic seeds are used as a spice. Also known as cardamon.

Cardinal: An entrée served with a wine sauce containing shrimp or lobster. The name derives from the red color of boiled crustaceans.

Carmine: A nontoxic substance derived from cochineal that is used to impart a vivid red color to food.

Carnitas (Sp.): A Mexican dish consisting of corn tortillas (q.v.) filled with chopped pork, chili powder, tomatoes, and seasonings.

Carob: A seed that grows in a pod. It is rich in sugar and protein and used as a chocolate substitute and is sometimes called St. John's Bread.

Carte, à la (Fr.): Refers to a restaurant meal in which the diner selects individual items, paying for each, rather than ordering a specific meal served complete at a fixed price. See also Table d'Hôte.

Cashew Nut: A white kidney-shaped nut with a buttery flavor.

Cassata (Ital.): A kind of Neapolitan ice cream; also an Italian cake.

Casserole: A stewpot or Dutch oven in which dishes of meat, game, fish, poultry, and/or vegetables are cooked very slowly in a liquid sauce, over direct heat or in the oven. Also denotes the food itself, e.g., beef casserole.

Cassis (Fr.): A liqueur made from black currants.

Cassoulet (Fr.): A famous French dish made with white beans and a combination of pork, poultry, sausage, and mutton cooked together in well-seasoned water.

Castor Sugar: English term for fine granulated sugar, similar to our superfine.

Catnip: A strong-scented herb of the mint family used in teas and for seasonings. Much favored by cats.

Catsup or Ketchup: A highly spiced preserved sauce of English origin, used as a condiment for meats or fish. Tomato catsup is the best known today, but catsups are also made from mushrooms, plums, elderberries, walnuts, and even lemons.*

*See *The Forgotten Art of Making Old-Fashioned Pickles, Relishes, Chutneys, Sauces and Catsups, Mincemeats, Beverages and Syrups.* Yankee, Inc., Dublin, N.H., 1978.

Caviar: The salted roe of sturgeon. Also applied to the roe of other fish, such as salmon ("red caviar") or lumpfish.

Cayenne: Dried, ground red pepper — the main seasoning in "hot" foods.

Celeriac: The turniplike variety of celery that is primarily root rather than stalks; also known as knob celery or celery root.

Celery Seed: The seed of the celery plant; used as a flavoring in soups, stews, stuffings, barbecue sauce, boiled dressing, and potato salad.

Cellulose: A more or less hard substance constituting the tissue of vegetable matter.

Cèpe (Fr.): A kind of edible mushroom.

Cerveza (Sp.): Mexican beer.

Chablis (Fr.): White burgundy wine from France.

Challah: Twisted loaves of white bread prepared for the Jewish Sabbath.

Champagne (Fr.): A sparkling white, usually dry, wine from the Champagne province of France. Its very name connotes luxury. Also applied to similar wines from other locations.

Chantilly (Fr.): Fresh cream whipped to a mousse consistency, then sweetened and flavored.

Chapon (Fr.): A slice of Italian or French bread rubbed with garlic, oil, and vinegar and added to salad greens to impart flavor. It can be eaten but is usually discarded.

Charcuterie (Fr.): The art of preparing various meats (particularly pork) in different ways. Also the name for the shops in France that specialize in selling such prepared meats (sausages, boned and rolled meats, pâtés, etc.).

Charlotte (Fr.): Usually a gelatin dessert of flavored Bavarian cream moulded in a form lined with sponge cake or ladyfingers.

Chartreuse (Fr.): A spicy, greenish liqueur made by the monks of Chartreux, France.

Chasseur (Fr.): "Hunter's style" — food with a robust sauce containing tomatoes, garlic, mushrooms, and red wine; also, food served garnished with mushrooms and shallots moistened with white wine.

Chateaubriand (Fr.): A thick slice of beef taken from the middle of the fillet, grilled, and served with béarnaise sauce (q.v.).

Chaud-Froid (Fr.): Literally, "hot-cold." A term for fowl, fish, or game cooked hot, then glazed with aspic or gelatin flavored with truffles and Madeira, and served cold.

Cheddar: A firm, classic English cheese of varying sharpness; excellent for cooking.

Cheese, Processed: A pasteurized cheese made from several kinds of natural cheese combined with emulsifying agents into a homogeneous plastic mass. Blander than natural, aged cheeses.

Chemise, en (Fr.): A term describing vegetables served with their skins on; also, small pieces of food wrapped in a thin layer of dough and baked.

Chervil: A potherb with stiff stems and curly leaves; used for seasoning.

Cheshire Cheese (Brit.): Its unusual flavor and texture come from the salty marsh grass eaten by Cheshire cows. Also known as Chester Cheese, Cheshire comes in two colors, red and white.

Chianti (Ital.): A well-known Italian red wine, produced chiefly in Tuscany.

Chickpea: A legume used in Spain for soups or served in North Africa with couscous (q.v.). It can be boiled until soft and served with sausage, or pureed and served, with various seasonings, in envelopes of unleavened bread.

Chicory: A herb used in salads. Its root is roasted for mixing with coffee.

Chiffonade (Fr.): Shredded plants or herbs, especially sorrel or lettuce, sautéed to garnish soups or used raw in salads.

Chilies: Small, hot red peppers from Mexico, used fresh, dried, or ground.

Chili Powder: Ground, dried chilies, used in hot and spicy sauces.

Chill: To refrigerate food or to let it stand in ice or ice water until cold.

Chine: The chine represents, in culinary terms, the bony part next to the fillet of a loin of lamb, mutton, pork, or veal; also the bony sector of a sirloin of beef.

Chinese Cabbage: A cross between romaine lettuce and cabbage; also known as celery cabbage or bok choy.

Chipolata: A garnish consisting of braised chestnuts, little glazed onions, diced sausage, glazed carrots, and breast of pork.

Chitterlings: Cooked animal intestines, popular in parts of the southern United States.

Chives: A perennial herb plant related to the onion and used to flavor soups, omelets, etc.

Chocolate: The solid or pliable mass obtained by grinding roasted, shelled cacao beans.

Choke: The inner prickly leaves, sharp and pale purple, in the core of an artichoke.

Chop: To cut into small pieces with a knife or an electric blender.

Chorizo (Sp.): A spicy Mexican sausage.

Chou(x) Paste: Cream-puff pastry made over heat in a saucepan.

Choucroute (Fr.): Sauerkraut.

Chowder: A soup or stew made of clams, fish, or vegetables and usually based on milk.

Chrysanthemum Leaves: Fragrant greens that are frequently used in stews, soups, and tempura (q.v.).

Chub: A variety of freshwater fish known in the United States as "longjaw," "blackfin," or "bloater," and found in the Great Lakes.

Chutney: A highly seasoned, preserved relish made of fruits and vegetables and served traditionally with curries.

Cider: A drink made from pressed apples. In Europe cider is fermented and sold commercially as a more or less alcoholic drink.

Cilantro: The parsleylike leaves of fresh coriander, used in Oriental cookery.

Cinnamon: A dried spice obtained from the bark of a tropical Asian tree. Available ground or as "cinnamon sticks" of rolled bark.

Citric Acid: An organic acid found in citrus fruits and used in making ades or syrups from those fruits.

Citron: A fruit grown for the peel only; it is like the lemon in appearance and structure. The candied peel is used as an ingredient in holiday breads, fruitcakes, and desserts.

Citronella: A coarse, lemon-scented plant of the mint family. The leaves of the plant are used for seasoning. Digestive liqueurs can be made from its flowers, and its extract is used as an insect repellent.

Clabber: Milk soured to a point where there is marked precipitation of curd but no separation from the whey. Buttermilk, sour milk, clabber, and yogurt may be used interchangeably in cooking.

Clafouti (Fr.): A thick pancake fruited with black cherries.

Clam: An edible bivalve mollusk, eaten either raw or cooked.

Claret: The English term for red Bordeaux wines.

Clarified Butter: Butter melted, then strained or skimmed to remove whitish sediment.

Clarify: To clear a liquid of bits of food or cloudy substances by adding egg white and eggshell and beating them in over heat. The broth is then strained; the food particles cling to the egg and are separated from the liquid.

Clove: A dried bud from the clove tree. Cloves are sold whole or ground and used as a spice.

18

Clove Oil: Oil distilled from clove flower buds and used for flavoring.

Coat: To cover all sides of food with another ingredient, such as flour or bread crumbs.

Coat the Spoon: The stage reached in cooking when a liquid mixture is thick enough to adhere in a thin layer to the bowl of the stirring spoon.

Cocoa Beans: The fruit of the cacao tree, grown as seeds in a pod, and the basis of cocoa and chocolate.

Cocotte (Fr.): Casserole-type utensil, either oval or round in shape, with a tightly fitting cover.

Cod: A large fish of the North Atlantic with white, flaky flesh and edible roe. Also known colloquially as "Cape Cod Turkey."

Cognac (Fr.): Brandy manufactured in the Cognac region of France; other brandies are not Cognac.

Cointreau (Fr.): A clear, orange-flavored, after-dinner liqueur.

Cold or Raw Pack: A method of preserving. The jars are filled with raw food and then processed in a water bath or steam-pressure canner.

Combine: To mix together two or more ingredients.

Comfits (Fr.): Fruits or vegetables preserved in sugar, brandy, or vinegar.

Compote: A dessert of fresh or dried fruits cooked in syrup. Also, a deep, often stemmed bowl in which such desserts or other foods are served.

Con Carne (Sp.): With meat.

Concasser (Fr.): To chop roughly or shred coarsely. Usually applied to tomatoes that have first been peeled, halved, then very gently squeezed to remove the seeds.

Conchiglie (Ital.): Small, rounded shells of pasta, available ridged or smooth.

Condiment: A highly seasoned sauce, such as catsup, A-1, or Worcestershire; or anything else used to season or flavor prepared foods. Loosely, the term can be extended to include all spices and flavorings.

Confectioners' Sugar: Refined white sugar ground to the consistency of cornstarch.

Confiture (Fr.): A jam, jelly, or conserve consisting basically of sugar and fruits.

Consommé (Fr.): An enriched meat stock that has been reduced (boiled down) and clarified (q.v.).

Convection Oven: An oven that cooks meals through a hot-air-in-motion system in less time and at lower temperatures than conventional ovens.

Cooking Liquor: A liquid broth in which meats, poultry, game, or vegetables have been cooked. Full of vitamins, it can be used as a stock in soups and stews, seasoned and served as an accompaniment to the food in which it was cooked (like clam liquor), or boiled down to intensify its flavor (like consommé) or produce a by-product (like starch, from potato cooking liquor).

Coq (Fr.): The French word for cock or rooster, but usually used in titles of French dishes to mean chicken.

Coq au Vin (Fr.): The classic French chicken dish cooked in wine with onions, herbs, garlic, and mushrooms.

Coquille (Fr.): A scallop or other shell in which food, usually creamed seafood or chicken, is served.

Coquille St. Jacques (Fr.): Creamed scallops served in a shell or coquille.

Coral: The roe of the female lobster, which reddens when cooked.

Cordon Bleu (Fr.): An award granted for excellence in cooking. Chicken or veal so described is stuffed with ham and cheese.

Core: To remove the center of a fruit or vegetable, leaving the rest intact.

Coriander: A herb widely cultivated for its aromatic seeds and used mainly as a condiment.

Cornet (Fr.): A slice of meat or bread or a square of thin pastry or cookie dough rolled into a cone shape.

Cornichon (Fr.): A gherkin or small pickled cucumber.

Cornmeal: Meal obtained by grinding corn; used for cooking and baking.

Corn Oil: Oil obtained from crushed corn, used as a cooking oil, for mayonnaise, or for salad dressing.

Cornstarch: A white flour milled from corn and used as a thickening agent.

Corn Sugar: Sugar manufactured from cornstarch.

Corn Syrup: A sweet syrup obtained by processing crude cornstarch.

Cottage Cheese: A soft, white cheese made of strained and seasoned curds of skim milk.

Coulibiac (Russ.): A hot fish pie usually made with salmon and kasha (buckwheat) and covered with a pastry dough.

Coulis (Fr.): Juices obtained from cooking various meats; also denotes certain thick soups made with fish purees.

Coupe (Fr.): A fruit cup served in a glass dish, often topped with ice cream.

Court-Bouillon (Fr.): A seasoned stock used as a liquid in which to cook fish; also, the liquor remaining after the fish has been cooked.

Couscous (Fr.): The North African or Arabian version of pilaf — i.e., a starch such as crushed millet, rice, or other grain cooked with meat.

Cracklings: The crisp residue left when fat, especially hog fat, is rendered; or the crisp, dark rind of pork roast.

Crack Stage: A candy-making term. One of the many different stages that boiled sugar syrup goes through before becoming caramel: 300°-310° F. (hard crack) or 270°-290° F. (soft crack).

Cranberry: A tart fruit resembling a small, dark-red cherry; can be used raw or cooked.

Cranberry Sauce: Stewed cranberries with sugar (and sometimes white or port wine); can be combined with oranges. Served in the United States with roast turkey or chicken.

Crayfish or Crawfish: A freshwater, lobsterlike crustacean used primarily in soups and stews. If you are lucky enough to have crayfish at hand, crayfish butter is a wonderful by-product.

Cream: To make a mixture soft and smooth by beating with a spoon or an electric mixer; usually refers to blending fat and sugar together. Another meaning is to cook food in, or serve it with, a white or cream sauce.

Cream Cheese: Soft, fresh cheese blended with cream to a smooth consistency. It is very bland and therefore it is often combined with other ingredients.

Crècy, à la (Fr.): A name given to various dishes, all of which include carrots.

Crème Brulée (Fr.): Caramel custard.

Crème Fraîche (Fr.): A matured cream whose lactic acids and natural ferments have been allowed to work until the cream has thickened and taken on a nutty flavor. American whipping cream or sour cream may be used in recipes calling for crème fraîche.

Crème Pâtissière (Fr.): A thick custard or cream used as a pastry filling.

Créole, à la (Fr.): Served in a spicy sauce containing tomatoes, onions, and peppers.

Crêpe (Fr.): A thin French pancake made of a batter of eggs, milk, and flour similar to that used for popovers or Yorkshire pudding. Served with butter and syrup or rolled around various fillings and sauced for a main dish or dessert.

Crêpes Suzette (Fr.): Crêpes made from a batter flavored with curaçao (q.v.) or orange juice, then cooked, rolled, and served with a hot orange sauce flavored with curaçao or brandy. Usually set aflame before serving.

Cress: Watercress.

Crimp: To gash around the edges with a sharp knife, as the fat around a ham slice; prevents meat from curling during broiling, roasting, or frying. Also, to press two layers of pastry together to seal, using a fork or a pastry wheel.

Crisp: To make a food firm and brittle by letting it stand in ice water or by heating it in the oven.

Croissant (Fr.): A flaky, butter-rich crescent-shaped roll made with a leavened dough repeatedly rolled out, spread with butter, folded, again rolled out, etc., before baking.

Croquembouche (Fr.): Literally, "crunch in your mouth" — a dessert made from small chou pastry puffs filled with cream, piled into a pyramid shape, and glazed with caramelized sugar. Traditional for Christmas or New Year's Day.

Croque-Monsieur (Fr.): A hot French-toast sandwich filled with lean ham and Gruyère cheese, and fried until golden brown on both sides in clarified butter. Served plain or with light cheese sauce.

Croquettes (Fr.): Patties made from a mixture of minced, ground, or chopped meat, fowl, vegetables, and rice bound with a thick white or brown sauce, coated with crumbs, eggs, then crumbs again, and fried in deep fat.

Croustade (Fr.): Denotes dishes consisting of flaky pastry or hollowed-out French bread enclosing fillings of different kinds.

Croûte, en (Fr.): Food that is enclosed or wrapped in a pastry crust before cooking.

Croutons (Fr.): Small cubes of bread, fried in butter or toasted until crisp, and served with soups or on salads, or as a garnish for various dishes.

Crudités (Fr.): Crisp, fresh, raw vegetables (broccoli or cauliflower flowerets, sliced carrots, radishes, tomatoes, etc.) served as an appetizer, often with a dip.

Crumb: To coat foodstuffs in bread crumbs or cracker crumbs that have been previously dipped in an adhesive liquid, such as beaten egg or pancake batter.

Crumble: To break into small pieces with the fingers.

Crust: The hard-baked outer part of bread or rolls; also, the pastry used to house a pie or tart.

Cube: To cut food into small cubes (about one-half inch square). Also, to score the surface of meat in a checkered pattern to increase its tenderness by breaking down tough fibers, as cubed beef.

Cubed Sugar: Crystals of granulated sugar pressed together into moulds and cut into cubes.

Cuisine (Fr.): Literally, "kitchen" — a style of cooking; i.e., American, Italian, et al., cuisines.

Cuisine Minceur (Fr.): A new approach to cooking that aims to reduce calories by reducing the fats and sugars.

Cumberland Sauce: A wine sauce flavored with red currant jelly, used cold or hot with ham or pork.

Cumin: A plant whose seeds are used ground or whole for seasoning.

Curaçao: An orange-flavored liqueur named after the island of Curaçao, located off the coast of Venezuela. Made in the Dutch West Indies and Holland.

Curd: A solid resulting from the coagulation of milk casein and separation of the liquid portion (whey). The separation may occur naturally as the milk sours, or the curd may be artificially precipitated by the addition of vinegar or rennet to fresh milk.

Curdle: Refers to the separation of a sauce or pudding made with eggs and a milk product into two parts — a liquid and the small solid particles floating in it. A curdled sauce or pudding may often be reclaimed by beating it slowly over low heat.

Cure: To preserve meat with salt, often allied with a smoking process.

Currant: The red, black, or greenish fruit of a prickly shrub; used chiefly to make jelly.

Curry: Food served in a heavily spiced sauce made with curry powder and served with rice and a number of special side dishes, or "boys" — peanuts, sieved hard-boiled egg yolks and whites, chutney, chopped onion, grated coconut, et al.

Curry Powder: A blend of commercially available pungent spices that gives curry (q.v.) its distinctive taste. Usually includes cumin, coriander, and turmeric.

Custard: Milk or cream mixed with eggs. Used with cheese, in a quiche, for example; or sweetened with sugar and flavored as a dessert or dessert sauce, as in baked or boiled custard.

Cut and Fold: To incorporate an ingredient such as beaten egg white or floured raisins lightly and evenly into a batter with a spoon, using a technique by which the spoon is sliced straight down to the bottom of the bowl, then drawn up along the bottom and side to fold the batter thereby scooped up over the top of the new ingredient.

Cut In: To blend flour with shortening by working the flour into the fat with a pastry blender or two knives.

Dab: A flat, white fish. All recipes for plaice are suitable for dab. See also flounder.

Damson: A variety of plum used in making jam.

Darjeeling: A variety of black Indian tea.

Decant: To pour any liquid from one container to another. Wine is decanted to get rid of the sediment deposited on the bottom of the wine bottle.

Deep-Fat Fryer: A deep, heavy pan with a wire basket that can be lowered into boiling fat during cooking.

Deep Fry: To cook in hot fat that is deep enough for food to float in.

Defrost: To thaw frozen foods.

Deglaze: To dilute and dissolve with hot liquid rich meat or poultry drippings, juices, and residue left in a pan in which meat or poultry has been cooked. The thus diluted juices, drippings, and residue are then used, strained or unstrained, to make sauce or gravy for the meat or poultry from which they came, or are saved and used in soup.

Degrease: To skim fat from the surface of hot liquids.

Dehydration: A process that removes the water content from foodstuffs.

Demi-Glaze (Fr.: Demi-Glace): A boiled-down, basic brown or espagnole sauce used as an ingredient in many different compound brown sauces.

Demitasse (Fr.): A small cup of black coffee, served after dinner.

Devil: To prepare with hot seasoning or sauce.

Devonshire Cream: English clotted cream, very rich and thick.

Diable Sauce: A sauce made of chopped shallots, pepper, white wine, cayenne pepper, meat stock, and tomato puree. Served with meats and turkey bones.

Dice: To cut into very small cubes — usually one-fourth inch square.

Dijon Mustard: Mustard prepared with white wine from a recipe originating in Dijon, France. May be either mild or sharp.

Dill or Dill Weed: A green herb used

minced, dried or fresh, as a flavoring. Particularly good combined with sour cream as a meat sauce.

Dill Seed: Seed of the dill plant or weed; used to flavor pickles and other foods.

Dilute: To thin by adding liquid, thus diminishing the strength or flavor of a mixture.

Dip: Usually a creamed, savory mixture served with crackers, potato chips, shrimp, or vegetables, as an hors d'oeuvre.

Diplomat Sauce: Normandy sauce (q.v.) with lobster butter, brandy, and cayenne and often including diced lobster meat and chopped truffles. Served with fish.

Disjoint: To separate at the joint, as with poultry or small game.

Dissolve: To melt or liquefy.

Dolma (Gr.): A combination of minced cooked lamb, rice, and vegetables wrapped and cooked in grape leaves.

Dot: To scatter bits of an ingredient such as butter or margarine over the surface of food.

Double Boiler: Two saucepans fitted into one another, the lower and larger one of which is filled with water at almost boiling point in order to cook or keep hot the food in the pan above without direct heat. See also Bain Marie.

Dough: A spongy mixture of flour, liquid, and other ingredients, thick enough to knead.

Dragées (Fr.): Tiny, spherical, silver candies used for decoration.

Drain: To strain liquid from solid food.

Drambuie: A Scotch-whiskey cordial flavored with honey.

Draw: To remove the entrails from poultry or game.

Drawn Butter: Clarified butter (q.v.).

Dredge: To coat or cover food with a dry ingredient, such as flour, corn-meal, or sugar.

Dress: To trim and clean fowl for cooking; also, to prepare the bird for the table by garnishing.

Dried Peas: There are three kinds commonly used in cooking: yellow or green peas, split or whole, and chickpeas (q.v.).

Dripping Pan: A pan placed under food while cooking to catch the juices and drippings.

Drippings: Fat, juices, and other residue left in a pan in which meat or poultry has been cooked; can be combined with flour and a liquid to make gravy, or deglazed (q.v.) and saved for sauces, gravy, or soup.

Drizzle: To pour melted butter, syrup, sauce, or other liquid in a fine stream in a zigzag pattern over the surface of food.

Dubonnet (Fr.): French apéritif wine.

Duchesse (Fr.): Describes potatoes mashed with cream and egg yolk, seasoned, and pressed through a pastry tube to form a decorative garnish.

Duck Press: A kitchen utensil used to extract the juices from a duck carcass.

Dumpling: A small ball of dough cooked on top of a soup or stew; can be sweetened, wrapped around fruit, baked, boiled, or steamed, and served as a dessert.

Dundee Cake: A rich fruitcake of Scottish origin, the top of which is covered with blanched almonds.

Dunlop: A creamy-textured Scottish cheese excellent for grilling or toasting, since it softens and browns without melting.

Dust: To sprinkle food with a dry ingredient such as flour or confectioners' sugar.

Dutch Oven: A heavy stewpot with a tight-fitting lid, used for making soups and stews and for braising; a "cocotte."

Duxelles (Fr.): A combination of finely chopped mushrooms, onions, shallots, salt, pepper, and nutmeg, lightly browned in butter — sort of a mushroom hash; used as a garnish or to fill mushroom caps.

23

Éclair (Fr.): An elongated piece of baked puff (chou) paste filled with flavored cream and spread with chocolate icing. See also Chou(x) Paste, Puff Pastry.

Edam: A famous Dutch cheese, usually made in the shape of a ball and coated with red wax.

Eel: A long, snakelike fish with a slippery skin and delicate flesh, which can be prepared in many ways.

Egg Coddler: A small china container with a screw-top metal lid. A raw egg is broken into it, and the container is placed in boiling water. The resulting cooked egg is served in the coddler.

Egg Cups: Cups especially designed to serve boiled eggs at table. A single boiled egg in its shell is served in the small end; one or two boiled eggs removed from the shell are served in the large end.

Eggnog: A drink made from egg yolks, milk, and sugar, flavored with vanilla or grated nutmeg, sometimes laced with rum or brandy. Also sometimes frothed with beaten egg whites.

Egg Poacher: A shallow, lidded, metal pan that holds water and is fitted with small, round containers, each large enough to hold a single egg.

Egg Separator: A device for separating the white of an egg from the yolk. The egg is broken into it, and the white slides out through a slit.

Egg Slicer: A small utensil that cuts a hard-boiled egg into uniform slices.

Egg Timer: A small hourglass that contains a fixed quantity of sand. When the timer is turned upside down, sand passes from top to bottom, taking three minutes, which is the usual time required to soft-boil an egg.

Elderberry: A berry used for making wine, pie, or jam.

Émincé (Fr.): A term used to describe very finely sliced meat, poultry, vegetables, or fruit.

Emmenthal (Ger.): A hard Swiss cheese made from whole milk. It has many holes or "eyes." Generally known as "Swiss cheese" in the United States.

En Brochette (Fr.): Food broiled on a skewer.

Enchilada (Sp.): A tortilla with filling and sauce.

En Papillote (Fr.): Baked in paper. The original French method was to encase food in an oiled-paper wrapping, but now aluminum foil is substituted.

Enriched: Food supplemented with vitamins and minerals lost or diminished during commercial processing.

Entrée (Fr.): The main course of an informal meal, or a subordinate dish served between main courses.

Entremets (Fr.): Literally, "between dishes." An entremets is usually a side dish. It may also be a dish served between the principal courses of a meal, or even as a dessert.

Epicure: A gourmet who is a connoisseur of food and wine.

Escabèche (Sp.): A pickled dish containing fish, meat, or poultry; popular in Latin countries.

Escalopes (Fr.): Thin slices of meat, chicken, or fish dipped in batter and fried. Known as "scallopini" in Italy, "schnitzel" in Germany, and "collops" in England.

Escargot (Fr.): An edible snail.

Escarole: A variety of salad green with wide, dark-green leaves, which are curled to a greater or lesser degree; used in conjunction with other salad greens, such as endive and chicory.

Espagnole Sauce: The basic brown sauce, made from meat drippings, mirepoix (q.v.), flour, tomatoes, pepper, parsley, and beef stock.

Essence: An oily or volatile liquid, extracted by distilling vegetable substances in water; i.e., essence of lemon, orange, etc.

Eviscerated or Drawn Poultry: Completely cleaned poultry. Generally, the gizzard, neck, heart, and liver (giblets) are removed and used to make stock or gravy.

Farci (Fr.): Stuffed with a meat, bread, rice, or other savory stuffing.

Farfalle (Ital.): A type of small pasta that is shaped like a bow tie.

Farfel: Minced noodle dough.

Farina: A general term for any meal or flour.

Farina Dolce (Ital.): Flour made from ground chestnuts.

Fat: The generic term for butter, margarine, lard, vegetable shortenings; also, the rendered drippings of meat, fowl.

Fava (Ital.): Large, white beans sold with or without their skins; can also refer to fresh green beans.

Fell: The thin, papery tissue on the outside surface of a leg of lamb.

Fennel: Herb with a flavor similar to that of aniseed. The large, fleshy bulb at the base of the stem is edible and is served both raw and cooked.

Fenugreek: An Asiatic herb with rather bitter but aromatic seeds, sometimes used in curry powder.

Fermentation: A chemical change, caused by bacterial action, that alters the characteristics of foodstuffs.

Feta Cheese: A crumbly, semisoft, white Greek cheese.

Fettuccine (Ital.): An egg noodle, narrower and thicker than tagliatelle (q.v.).

Filbert: A hazelnut.

Filé: A powder made from ground sassafras leaves; added to a stew or gumbo just before serving.

Fillet, Filet: To remove the bone; also a boneless piece of meat or fish.

Filo or Phyllo Pastry: A flaky, rich, paper-thin pastry dough of Greek origin, used for sweets and savories.

Filter: To strain liquid through porous (filter) paper or several thicknesses of cheesecloth.

Fines Herbes (Fr.): A mixture of finely chopped fresh or dried herbs, such as chives, parsley, tarragon, and chervil.

Finish: To prepare a dish for the table by garnishing.

Finnan Haddie: Smoked haddock.

Finocchio (Ital.): Fennel (q.v.).

Firm-Ball Stage: When hot sugar syrup dropped into cold water forms a ball that will hold its shape upon removal from the water, the temperature of the boiling syrup has reached 244°-248° F.

Five-Spice Powder: An aromatic blend of cinnamon bark, star anise, anise pepper, fennel, and cloves, used in Chinese cookery.

Flake: To separate cooked fish into small pieces or flakes, removing any bones.

Flambé (Fr.): A term used to describe food covered or combined with spirits, set alight, and served flaming.

Flan: A pie or tart shell enclosing a cream, fruit, or savory filling. Also, a moulded custard dessert served with a caramelized sauce.

Flatten: To flatten and thin a piece of meat by pounding it with a beater, mallet, or the back of a heavy frying pan, thus tenderizing it and reducing the time required to cook it.

Florentine: Food served with or on a bed of spinach, often creamed; also, a kind of cookie.

Floret: A small flower, usually one of a large cluster of composite flowers, as in broccoli or cauliflower.

Flounder: A flat, white-fleshed fish of the same family as the sole.

Flour: A fine meal made of ground cereal grains, such as wheat or rye. Also, to sprinkle food that is to be deep-fried lightly with flour; or to dip food in flour before dipping it in egg and bread crumbs.

Flour Sifter: A sieve especially designed for sifting flour.

Fluff: To fork up until light and fluffy; also, a spongy gelatin dessert.

Flute: A term used to describe the operation of cutting or scoring vegetables and fruits, or shaping the edge of a pastry shell in a decorative manner.

Foie Gras (Fr.): A preparation made from the enlarged livers of specially fattened geese and ducks. The finest comes from France.

Fold in: See Cut and Fold.

Fondant: A creamy sugar paste that is kneaded until smooth and used as an icing or candy.

Fondue: A Swiss dish composed of cheese melted with wine or brandy and used for dipping. Also a dessert made of melted sweet chocolate, a soufflélike dessert, and cubes of beef cooked in hot fat at the table.

Fontina (Ital.): A delicate, semisoft Italian cheese.

Food Chopper: A crescent-shaped knife with handles on both ends, employed with a rocking motion to chop or dice fruits and vegetables. See also Mezzaluna.

Food Mill: A device that forces fruits and vegetables through small perforations to produce pureed or riced particles.

Food Processor: An electric utensil with attachments that chop, mix, slice, and shred.

Fool: A fruit puree mixed with thick whipped cream.

Forcemeat: Finely minced or ground meat, fowl, game, or fish, used as a stuffing or filling, or as a garnish.

Fortified: Supplied with more vitamins and minerals than were present in the natural state.

Fra Diavolo (Ital.): Describes a lobster dish made with tomatoes.

Framboise (Fr.): Raspberry.

Frangipane (Fr.): A sweet pastry cream.

Freeze: To chill until solid.

French Fry: To cook in deep, hot fat until brown and crisp.

Fricassee: Pieces of meat, particularly chicken or veal, stewed or fried, and served in a sauce (usually, but not always, white) made from the gravy.

Frijoles (Sp.): Mexican beans.

Frit, Frite (Fr.): Fried food. French fried potatoes are known as "frites" in France.

Frittata (Ital.): Omelet.

Frittelle (Ital.): Pancakes.

Fritter: Food dipped in batter to coat and then fried.

Fritto-Misto (Ital.): Pieces of meat and vegetables coated with batter and deep-fat fried.

Frizzle: To fry food in hot fat until the edges curl.

Fromage, au (Fr.): With cheese.

Frost: To cover with sugar icing.

Fructose: Natural sugar found in fruit.

Fry: To cook in fat, either shallow, as in pan-frying, or deep, as in deep-fat frying.

Fumet (Fr.): Stock obtained by boiling fish, meat, or vegetables in water, stock, or wine, which is then reduced and intensified in flavor by being boiled down.

Fusilli (Ital.): Long, spirally twisted spaghetti.

Galantine (Fr.): A cold preparation of boned, stuffed, and seasoned chicken, veal, or fish, usually covered with aspic and chilled in decorative moulds.

Gallimaufry: A medieval cooking term meaning a stew. Nowadays, it is used in a disparaging sense to mean a hodgepodge.

Galuptze (Russ.): Chopped meat rolled in cabbage leaves.

Game: A general term used to describe edible wild birds or animals not usually raised for food.

Garlic: A perennial plant of the *Allium* (onion) family, distinguished by its strong odor, cultivated for its bulb, and used in all kinds of cooking.

Garnish: To decorate a dish by adding small amounts of food or herbs for color or flavor; also the food or herb so used.

Gâteau (Fr.): Cake.

Gaufrette (Fr.): A thin, wafflelike wafer.

Gazpacho (Sp.): A cold soup or salad made with tomatoes, cucumbers, onions, sweet peppers, and herbs.

Gefilte Fish: Literally, "stuffed fish." A traditional Jewish dish made from a combination of pike, white fish, onions, and seasonings, bound together with eggs, and then poached. Served hot or cold.

Gelatin: A colorless, tasteless solid obtained by boiling bones, cartilage, and tendons. Mixed with hot water, the commercially available product renders liquids viscous and, when chilled, turns them into a jelly.

Gelato (Ital.): Ice cream.

Gelée, en (Fr.): Food moulded in jelly or glazed with aspic.

Genevoise Sauce: An espagnole sauce (q.v.) based on fish stock with red wine and fish fumet (q.v.) added. Served chiefly with salmon and trout.

Gervais: A small, cylindrical, creamy French cheese.

Gherkin: Very young cucumbers of certain varieties especially suited for pickling. Gherkins are picked green.

Giblets: The edible viscera of poultry, such as the heart, liver, and gizzard.

Gigot (Fr.): Leg of lamb.

Gin: A spirit distilled from grain (barley, wheat, or oats) and flavored with juniper berries.

Ginger: A pungent root that comes dried in pieces, ground, candied, or in syrup; a flavoring.

Ginger Beer: English drink with a distinct ginger flavor.

Gjetöst (Nor.): Brown Norwegian goat cheese.

Glacé (Fr.): Denoting iced, glazed, or frozen foods.

Glace de Viande (Fr.): A concentrated meat glaze made by reducing strong brown stock to a jelly-like consistency; used to flavor and color.

Glacéed Fruit: Candied fruit or fruit peel.

Glaze: To coat with aspic or with a thin sugar syrup.

Gluten: An albuminous substance found in flour. The smooth, elastic properties of gluten are developed in bread dough by kneading.

Gnocchi (Ital.): Light dumplings made of flour or potatoes and eggs.

Gorgonzola (Ital.): A creamy, butter-yellow Italian cheese with green veins.

Gouda (Du.): A Dutch cheese made from whole milk.

Goulash: A thick Hungarian meat stew made with onions and flavored generously with paprika.

Grand Marnier (Fr.): An orange-flavored French liqueur used in fruit desserts and for flavoring sauces.

Granulated Sugar: Refined, small-crystalline, beet or cane sugar.

Grappa (Ital.): A highly alcoholic brandy flavored with rue and distilled from wine sediment.

Grate: To rub food on a rough surface, or chop in a blender or food processor, so as to produce fine, medium, or coarse particles.

Gratin, au (Fr.): Food topped with bread crumbs and butter or cheese, then baked or broiled until it acquires a golden brown crust.

Gratiner (Fr.): To brown the top of a sauced dish under the broiler with a sprinkling of bread crumbs, cheese, and butter.

Gravy: A sauce made from meat juices and fat thickened with flour, browned, then diluted with water; sometimes seasoned with herbs or spices.

Grease: To rub the surface of a dish or pan with shortening or other fat to keep food from sticking.

Green Olives: Green fruit of the olive tree, treated with a hot, weak, alkali solution, then pickled in brine.

Grenadine: A sugar syrup made from pomegranates or red currants used to sweeten or flavor foods or drinks.

Grenouilles (Fr.): Frogs' legs.

Gribiche Sauce: A cold sauce made from pulverized hard-boiled egg yolks beaten with oil and vinegar and mixed with chopped gherkins, capers, herbs, and julienne-cut egg whites. Used for cold fish or shellfish.

Grill: To cook over or under direct heat. Also a utensil or appliance used for this type of cooking.

Grind: To reduce food to tiny particles.

Grinder: A kitchen utensil that reduces food to small pieces or powder.

Grog: A hot drink containing rum or some other spirit plus lemon, sugar, and water.

Gruyère (Fr.): A creamy Swiss table and cooking cheese with a fine-grained, rather firm texture.

Guacamole (Sp.): A Mexican sauce or spread made from mashed avocados, with a little tomato pulp and lemon or onion juice.

Guava: The fruit of the tropical guava tree. Can be eaten raw, but is usually made into jam, jelly, or paste.

Gumbo: A thick, Southern-style soup made with meat, poultry, fish, shellfish, and vegetables, usually including okra.

Haché (Fr.): Hashed or minced.

Haddock: A white-fleshed fish of the cod family, frequently smoked (finnan haddie). Can be successfully used in all recipes specifying cod.

Haggis: A traditional Scottish dish consisting of a sheep's stomach filled with the minced heart, liver, and lungs, along with oatmeal and chopped suet.

Half and Half: A mixture of equal parts of milk and cream.

Half-Glaze Sauce: See Demi-Glaze.

Hang: To age game or meat by hanging in a cool, unrefrigerated place.

Hard-Ball Stage: When hot sugar syrup dropped into cold water forms a hard ball that will hold its shape, but is still pliable if pressed between thumb and finger, the temperature of the syrup is 250°-266° F.

Hard-Crack Stage: Hot sugar syrup dropped into cold water will separate into hard, brittle threads at a temperature of 300°-310° F.

Hard Sauce: A mixture of butter and confectioners' sugar kneaded together. Served with fruit desserts, Christmas puddings, or mince pies.

Haricot (Fr.): French word for bean; also used to describe a thick meat stew.

Hash: A dish usually made from minced or diced leftover roasted meats and vegetables.

Haute Cuisine (Fr.): Gourmet cooking.

Havarti (Dan.): A mild, creamy, white cheese.

Head Space: A canning term meaning the amount of space left between the food and any added liquid and the top of the jar.

Herb: Any plant whose leaves, root, or

stems are used as a food or to flavor food.

Hibachi (Jap.): A small, portable grill for table cooking.

Hock: General term for Rhine wines.

Hoisin Sauce: A thick, dark sauce made of soybeans, chili, spices, and garlic, used in Chinese cookery.

Hollandaise Sauce: A sauce made with egg yolks, butter, peppercorns, and lemon juice or vinegar.

Homard (Fr.): Lobster.

Hominy: Finely ground, parched corn, usually white.

Homogenization: Term used to describe the breaking down of fat into such small particles that it stays suspended in a liquid, rather than rising to the top.

Honey: A sweet liquid manufactured by bees, which can be used in the place of sugar. Substitute an equivalent volume of honey for sugar in baking breads or rolls; use only seven-eighths of a cup of honey to every cup of sugar in cakes or cookies, and reduce the amount of liquid by three tablespoons for each cup of honey used.

Hongroise (Fr.): Food cooked Hungarian-style.

Hors d'Oeuvres: Relishes or small appetizers served before the main dishes. The terms "hors d'oeuvres," "canapés," and "appetizers" are used interchangeably.

Horseradish: Horseradish root has a very sharp flavor; it is usually grated and served as a condiment, particularly with cold roast beef.

Hotch-Potch: Sometimes called hodge-podge — a soup or broth having so many ingredients that it resembles a stew.

Hot Pack: A canning method in which jars are filled with precooked hot food, then processed in a water bath or steam-pressure canner.

Hot Pot: A dish containing meat or fish cooked in layers in a special pot.

Hull: To strip or remove, as strawberry stems.

Hummus: A creamy dish of pureed chickpeas and sesame paste.

Ice: To chill in a refrigerator or over ice; also, a smooth frozen mixture of sweetened fruit juice.

Icing: Sugar frosting.

Impératrice, à la (Fr.): Term denoting cold rice pudding flavored with vanilla and crystallized fruit soaked in kirsch.

Impériale, à la (Fr.): Describes dishes garnished with kidneys, truffles, or foie gras.

Indienne, à l' (Fr.): Indian-style; generally applied to curries or dishes containing curry.

Infusion: The liquid that results from steeping tea, coffee, or herbs in boiling water.

Instant Flour: A granular flour having the consistency of finely granulated sugar or salt. Its only advantage over regular flour is that it dissolves more easily in sauces and gravies.

Italienne, à l' (Fr.): Italian-style; usually, a dish containing macaroni or noodles and tomato sauce, and served with Parmesan cheese and/or finely chopped or diced mushrooms.

Jambalaya: A traditional Creole dish combining rice with meat, fish, or shellfish.

Jar: A glass container made for canning use. There are three kinds: (1) the Mason jar that has a screw-thread neck and a sloping shoulder and is sealed at the top or at the shoulder, depending upon the type of cap used; (2) the tapered, shoulderless jar that may be used for either home canning or freezing, and is sealed on the top with a two-piece metal cap; and (3) the Lightning jar, sealed with a glass lid and a rubber ring held in place with a wire bail.

Jardinière, à la (Fr.): Prepared or garnished with vegetables.

Jell: To congeal with gelatin; also, to cook into a jelly.

Jelly-Roll Style: Rolled up around a filling.

Jeroboam: See table, "Oversize Wine Bottles," p. 61.

Jicama (Sp.): A crisp root vegetable from Mexico, eaten cooked or raw.

Jigger: A liquid measure equivalent to one and one-half fluid ounces.

Johnnycake (Jonnycake): Corn bread made from cornmeal water-ground from white or yellow corn.

Joint: To sever at the joint; also, a roasting cut of meat.

Julienne (Fr.): Cut into long, very narrow strips, as meats, vegetables, cheeses, etc.

Junket: The trade name for a dessert made from milk thickened with rennet, sweetened, and flavored.

Jus, au (Fr.): Term describing meat served with natural pan juices, seasoned, but not thickened with flour.

Kadota: A type of fig.

Kalamata Olives: Large, oval Greek olives with a smooth purple skin.

Kartoffel Kloese (Ger.): Potato dumplings or potato croquettes.

Kasha (Russ.): A cooked buckwheat cereal.

Kasseri (Gr.): A cheese made from sheep's milk. Has a strong, slightly winy flavor and somewhat grainy texture.

Kebab: Pieces of meats and vegetables arranged on a skewer and grilled.

Kedgeree: An English breakfast dish of fish creamed with rice and hard-boiled eggs.

King, à la: Food served in a rich cream sauce containing diced pimientos, and often chopped mushrooms or peppers.

Kipper: Split smoked herring served hot with butter and lemon juice, usually for breakfast.

Kirsch (Ger.): A dry brandy made from the pits of black cherries; used on fruits and in fruit desserts.

Kisses: Miniature meringues or other small candies.

Kitchen Bouquet: Trade name for a dark-brown bottled liquid used to add color and flavor to meat sauces, gravies, and stews.

Kiwi: A small, potatolike fruit with a juicy, green pulp.

Knead: To work dough, particularly bread dough, with the hands, folding and pressing repeatedly until the dough is smooth and elastic. See Gluten.

Kohlrabi: Also called kale turnip, this is a bizarre-looking cole vegetable with an edible, bulbous stem. Can be used interchangeably with turnips or celeriac.

Kola Nut: The bitter fruit of a Brazilian tree, used in preparing cola drinks.

Kosher: Foods whose preparation renders them ritually fit for consumption according to Jewish law.

Kreplach: Squares of noodle dough stuffed with meat, cheese, or other fillings and cooked in soup or sautéed.

Kuchen (Ger.): Cake, specifically a coffee cake.

Kugel: A starch pudding of Jewish origin made from noodles or potatoes.

Kulich (Russ.): A high, cylindrical cake made of a sweet bread dough rich in eggs and candied fruit; the traditional Russian Easter cake served with paskha (q.v.); similar to panettone (q.v.).

Kummel (Ger.): A liqueur prepared from caraway seeds.

Kumquat: A tiny orange shaped like an elongated olive, which can be candied or eaten raw in salads. Also used to make jam or marmalade.

Lactose: A sugar present in milk; used in medicines and foods.

Ladle: A large spoon with a long handle and cupped bowl; used primarily to serve or dip out liquids.

Lager: Any light beer.

Lait, au (Fr.): Food prepared or served with milk, e.g., café au lait.

Langue-de-Chat (Fr.): A crisp cookie baked from dough piped through a pastry bag onto the baking sheet in the form of a flat, narrow finger said to resemble a cat's tongue.

La Nouvelle Cuisine (Fr.): The new wave of French cooking that minimizes the use of fats, starches, and sugar. It was originated by Paul Bocuse in his restaurant at Collonges, near Lyons, France.

Lard: To cover meat with strips of fat, or to insert fat strips into meat to add flavor and prevent it from drying out during baking or roasting.

Larding Needle: A needle used to insert lardoons into meat or poultry. See Lardoon.

Lardoon: A long, thin strip of bacon, pork, or ham fat used to lard lean meats. Also called lardon. See Lard.

Larousse Gastronomique: A comprehensive encyclopedia of food, wine, and cookery in general, particularly French.

Lasagne (Ital.): Broad egg noodles.

Leaven: To raise dough by adding a lightening agent such as yeast, baking powder, or eggs.

Le Banon (Fr.): One of the best of a large family of small goat cheeses.

Leek: Edible, onionlike plant with flat leaves and a comparatively mild flavor; used as a vegetable and in soups.

Legumes: Large, podded, edible seeds such as peas, beans, and lentils.

Lemon Balm: Herb with lemon-scented leaves, whose sprigs are used for tea or cool drinks.

Lentils: Seeds of the lentil plant; a starchy, leguminous food high in protein.

Liaison: A flour mixture of egg yolks and cream used to thicken or bind sauces, soups, etc.

Lichee Nut: Also spelled "litchi" or "lychee." The fruit of the Chinese lichee tree is about the size of a cherry, with white, sweet pulp that can be dried or preserved. Used in Chinese cookery.

Lid: A round, flat cover of metal or glass used with a screw band or wire bail to seal a jar.

Liederkranz (Ger.): A strong and somewhat smelly native cheese.

Limburger (Flem.): A cheese which is semihard and fermented; known for its pungent odor.

Lime: The tart fruit of the lime tree, similar to a lemon but green in color.

Line: To cover the inside of a mould or baking dish with waxed paper, crumbs, etc., before adding food to be cooked.

Linguine (Ital.): A flat spaghetti.

Liptauer (Hung.): A simple, milk-curd Hungarian cheese with a sharp, sour-milk flavor.

Liqueur (Fr.): A sweet, syrupy alcoholic beverage.

Liquor: The liquid extracted from a food during cooking in water, such as oyster or clam broth, or the by-product of fermented grains; also, alcoholic spirits, such as rum, gin, whiskey, et al.

Loaf: A moulded mass of foodstuffs cooked together, as bread and meat in a meat loaf.

Loaf Sugar: Same as cubed sugar (q.v.), but differently shaped.

Lobster à l'Américaine: A dish prepared with lobster, tomatoes, garlic, chopped parsley, and tarragon.

Loganberry: A berry obtained by crossing blackberries and raspberries.

Loin: The front part of a hindquarter of lamb, pork, or veal, with the flank removed.

Loquat: The edible fruit of the loquat tree, native to Far-Eastern Asia.

Lotus Root: A crisp, crunchy, root vegetable with a mild, sweet flavor; used in Chinese cookery.

Low-Acid Foods: Foods that contain very little natural acid — all vegetables other than rhubarb, tomatoes, and sauerkraut, along with poultry and seafood.

Lukewarm: At a temperature of about 95° F. lukewarm food will feel neither warm nor cold when sprinkled on or held to the inside of the wrist.

Macadamia Nuts: Buttery, roasted, nutlike seeds of the macadamia tree; high in fat content.

Macaroni (Ital.): A general term for all dried pasta.

Macaroon: A small, cookielike pastry made of almond paste or shredded coconut, sugar, and egg whites.

Mace: The edible outer covering of nutmeg that is ground for use as a spice.

Macedoine (Fr.): Mixed fruits or vegetables cut into various shapes and sizes.

Macerate: To soften or soak foods in liquid. This term is usually reserved for fruits, as opposed to "marinate," which is used primarily for meats.

Macéré (Fr.): Steeped in wine or pickled.

Mackerel: A long, narrow, saltwater fish. A rather fatty fish, it can be eaten fresh, salted, or smoked.

Madeira Sauce: A combination of Madeira wine, stock, butter, and concentrated espagnole sauce (q.v.); served with meats.

Madeira Wine: A fortified wine made from grapes grown on the island of Madeira; used in cooking or as an apéritif.

Madeleine (Fr.): A small cake.

Madrilène (Fr.): Clear consommé flavored with tomato juice and usually served cold.

Mafalde (Ital.): A broad noodle with rippled edges.

Maggi Sauce: A concentrated commercial bottled meat sauce; used to enrich sauces, stews, and broths.

Magnum: See table, "Oversize Wine Bottles," p. 61.

Maître d'Hôtel (Fr.): Term used to describe dishes cooked quickly and plainly, with parsley as the main flavor. Also refers to the headwaiter or man in charge of the dining room.

Maize: British word for corn. In England, "corn" means oats. Also, in the United States, corn.

Malt: Barley prepared for brewing beer.

Mandarin Orange: A popular and inexpensive Oriental fruit.

Mango: An oblong yellow-orange fruit about the size of a large pear, eaten raw or made into jam or marmalade.

Manicotti (Ital.): Giant tubes of pasta, often stuffed with meat fillings.

Manzanilla Wine: A kind of sherry.

Maple Sugar: Crystallized maple syrup.

Maraschino: A liqueur made chiefly from a type of black cherry; also, red cherries preserved in syrup and used as decorations.

Marbled: Describes meat streaked with fat. This is most desirable.

Marinade: A seasoned liquid mixture, usually containing oil and an acid such as wine or vinegar, in which food is soaked to gain extra flavor or to be tenderized.

Marinara (Ital.): "Sailor fashion;" a quickly prepared sauce, usually consisting of tomatoes, onions, chopped carrots, and garlic.

Marinate: To soak in a marinade (q.v.) or salad dressing for whatever time — from a few hours to several days — required by the recipe.

Marjoram: An aromatic herb used to enhance pasta or egg dishes, as well as sauces and other foods.

Marmite (Fr.): A heavy kettle or earthenware pot.

Marrons Glacés (Fr.): Candied chestnuts preserved in sugar syrup.

Marrow: The fatty filling of beef leg bones, used in sauces, on canapés, or sliced as a garnish. See also Bone Marrow.

Marsala (Ital.): A sweet dessert wine made from grapes grown in Sicily; an essential ingredient of dishes such as Veal Marsala and Sabayon, or Zabaglione (q.q.v.).

Marzipan: A confection made from ground almonds, sugar, and egg whites; often shaped and tinted to resemble fruits and vegetables.

Masa (Sp.): A dough made from ground corn; used to make tortillas and tamales.

Mash: To reduce to a pulp with a fork or potato masher.

Mask: To cover completely with a sauce, jelly, aspic, mayonnaise, or cream.

Matelote (Fr.): A rich fish stew made with white or red wine.

Matelote Sauce: A mixture of fish stock, red wine, mushrooms, and demiglaze (q.v.), sieved and served with fish.

Matzos: Slices of thin, unleavened, crackerlike bread made of flour and water.

Matzos Ball: A dumpling made of matzos meal and eggs.

Mayonnaise: A cold sauce made of egg yolks, olive oil, wine vinegar, and seasonings; served with chicken, fish, eggs, and salads.

Meal: Grain ground to a powder.

Meat Glaze: The same as glace de viande (q.v.). Bovril and B-V are commercial versions of this beef extract.

Médaillon (Fr.): A small, round cut of meat or fish.

Mélange (Fr.): A mixture; usually applied to a combination of fruits.

Melba: A sauce made from fresh raspberries and sugar.

Melba Toast: Very thin slices of bread baked until crisp in a slow oven.

Melt: To use heat to turn a solid food into a liquid.

Meringue: A combination of beaten egg whites and sugar baked in various shapes or used as a pie topping.

Mescal (Sp.): Distilled Mexican liquor made from the century plant.

Methuselah: See table, "Oversize Wine Bottles," p. 61.

Mezzaluna (Ital.): A food chopper with a curved, nine-inch blade and wooden knob handles at either end.

Microwave: A cooking process in which heat energy is conducted through prepared food to cook it rapidly.

Milanèse, à la (Fr.): Food dipped in egg and bread crumbs and cooked in butter.

Mill: A small machine used to grind foodstuffs such as coffee, bread crumbs, pepper, etc.

Mille-Feuille (Fr.): Very thin, many-layered, flaky pastry.

Milt: Reproductive gland of male fish.

Mince: To cut into very small pieces, using a knife, food grinder, or blender.

Mincemeat: A combination of suet, raisins, currants, apples, sugar, brandy or rum, and several spices, usually steeped for a month or more; a traditional filling for holiday pies.

Minceur, Cuisine (Fr.): "Slimming cookery" utilizing the natural fats and sugars.

Minestrone (Ital.): A thick soup of beans, vegetables, and pasta.

Mint: A fragrant herb used as an ingredient in a large number of liqueurs and in cooking as a flavoring.

Mint Sauce: Chopped mint, lightly sweetened, seasoned, and moistened with vinegar; served with lamb.

Mirepoix (Fr.): Diced or chopped carrots, onions, and celery cooked in butter with thyme and used to add flavor to sauces or pot roasts.

Miso (Jap.): Soybean paste.

Mix: To combine or blend.

Mixed Pickling Spice: A blend of herbs and spices used in pickling.

Mocha: Describes a coffee or a combined coffee-and-chocolate flavor. Also a choice variety of coffee grown in Mocha, Arabia.

Mode, à la (Fr.): Literally, "in fashion." Desserts à la mode are served with ice cream; meats à la mode are braised with vegetables and served with gravy.

Molasses: A thick, brown, sweet syrup that does not crystallize; a by-product of sugar refining.

Mole: A concoction or sauce made with chilies.

Monosodium Glutamate: A white, water-soluble powder used to intensify the flavor of meats, vegetables, and other foods; commonly known as M.S.G.

Monterey Jack: A smooth, semisoft, and rather bland American cheese; excellent for melting.

Montmorency, à la (Fr.): A term describing cakes or sweets with cherries added in one form or another.

Morel: A small, edible mushroom.

Mornay Sauce: Béchamel sauce (q.v.) mixed with butter, cream, and grated Gruyère and Parmesan cheese.

Mortadella (Ital.): A large sausage, similar to the American bologna.

Mortar and Pestle: A mortar is a bowl or container in which foods are ground or crushed with the pestle, a clublike utensil.

Moselle: White wine from the Moselle River Valley.

Mostaccioli (Ital.): Obliquely cut, medium-size pasta tubes.

Mould (or Mold): Container used to form foods in its shape. Also, a jelled mixture shaped by a mould, such as an aspic ring.

Moussaka: Main dish of Rumanian origin, made with ground meat (preferably lamb), eggplant, tomatoes, onions, and seasonings.

Mousse: A frozen dessert of flavored gelatin and whipped cream; also, a moulded dish of creamed, minced food stiffened with gelatin, as ham mousse.

Mozzarella (Ital.): A rubbery, white Italian cheese that melts easily.

Muddler: A thick glass rod used to crush fruit and sugar in drinks.

Mull: To heat fruit juices, wine, ale, or other alcoholic beverages with sugar and spices.

Mulligatawny: A highly spiced Creole chicken dish made with curry powder; also, a curried East-Indian meat soup.

Münster (Ger.): A semihard, fermented whole-milk cheese. It can be flavored with caraway or aniseed.

Muscat: A type of grape.

Mushroom: A brown, fleshy fungus with an umbrellalike shape. Some types of mushroom are eminently edible, others doubtfully so, and quite a number are downright poisonous.

Mustard: A sharp condiment (q.v.) prepared from mustard seeds.

Mustard Sauce: Hollandaise sauce (q.v.) heavily flavored with mustard.

Mustard Seed: Seed used in pickling. When powdered, it is called English mustard; when blended with wine or vinegar, it is called French mustard.

Normandy Sauce: Velouté sauce (q.v.) made from fish stock and cream boiled down and supplemented with fish fumet (q.v.), mushroom, mussel, or oyster stock, and egg yolks.

Nougat: A candy made from sugar or honey syrup and nuts.

Nacho: Mexican appetizer made with chilies, cheese, and tortillas.

Nantua Sauce: A béchamel sauce (q.v.) flavored with crayfish (or shrimp) butter or puree.

Nasturtium: A decorative and edible plant. Its flowers and young leaves are used in salads, and the buds and seeds can be pickled like capers.

Naturel, au (Fr.): Uncooked, or cooked in a very simple manner.

Neapolitan Ice Cream: An ice-cream block consisting of a layer each of chocolate, strawberry, and vanilla.

Nebuchadnezzar: See table, "Oversize Wine Bottles," p. 61.

Nesselrode Pudding: A frozen, chestnut-flavored Bavarian cream.

Neufchâtel (Fr.): A soft, white cheese, similar to cream cheese but lower in calorie content.

Newburg: Diced, cooked lobster or seafood in a rich cream sauce flavored with sherry or Madeira.

Niçoise, à la (Fr.): Describes dishes made with black olives, anchovies, tomatoes, garlic, and olive oil.

Noggin: One-half cup of alcoholic spirits.

Noisette (Fr.): Literally, "hazelnut" — in cooking, refers to a small, round slice of meat, an individual portion.

Noisette Potatoes: Small, round balls cooked in butter until slightly browned.

Oats: A cereal grain rich in phosphorus, iron, and vitamins. Ground oats or oatmeal is used to make breads, cookies, porridge, and soups.

Oil: A liquid cooking fat pressed from peanuts, corn, cottonseed, sesame seed, poppy seed, or olives.

Okra: Edible vegetable pods, popular in southern and Creole cooking.

Oleomargarine: An artificial product made from solid vegetable fat and used as a substitute for butter.

Olives: The hard-stoned fruit of the olive tree, preserved for eating or pressed to produce olive oil.

Orange-Flower Water: A liquid containing essence of distilled orange blossoms; used for flavoring.

Orecchiette (Ital.): The name means "little ear," which is what the small, shell-shaped pasta looks like.

Oregano: Wild marjoram, a herb used lavishly in Italian cooking.

Osso Buco (Ital.): Literally "hollow bone" — a dish of veal marrow bones braised in wine and stock with tomatoes and onions, and served with rice.

Ouzo (Gr.): Anise-flavored apéritif.

Oyster: A bivalve mollusk, eaten either raw or cooked and considered a delicacy.

Oyster Plant: Also known as salsify, the plant has an edible root alleged to taste like oyster.

Oyster Sauce: A thick, oyster-flavored

sauce, used especially in Chinese cookery.

Oysters Casino: Oysters topped with lemon juice, bacon, and minced green pepper, and broiled on the half-shell.

Oysters Rockefeller: Oysters topped with seasoned, chopped spinach, bacon, and bread crumbs, and baked.

Paella (Sp.): A classic dish consisting of seafoods, chicken, rice, herbs, seasonings, and spices.

Pain (Fr.): Bread.

Panada (Fr.): A home-style soup consisting of bread soaked in milk, stock, or other liquid with butter and an egg or two. Also refers to a paste of flour, bread, or toast used for binding ground meat.

Pan Broil: To cook uncovered in a skillet with little or no fat, pouring off any fat rendered from food.

Pan Fry: See Fry.

Panettone (Ital.): A tall coffee cake made of a rich, sweet yeast dough containing raisins and candied fruit.

Papillotes (Fr.): Decorative frilled paper "petticoats" slipped over the ends of chop bones.

Pappadum (Ind.): Light, crisp flat breads.

Paprika (Hung.): A bright-red seasoning made from ground, dried red peppers.

Parboil: To boil until partially cooked.

Parch: To dry corn or other starchy vegetables by roasting.

Pare: To trim the skin, peel, or other outer covering from food with a knife or vegetable parer.

Parfait (Fr.): A dessert made of layers of fruit, syrup, ice cream, and whipped cream, frozen and served in a tall, slender glass.

Parmentier (Fr.): A dish including potatoes in some form.

Parmesan: A rock-hard, very pungent, sharp grating cheese; the very essence of Italian cooking.

Parsley: A hardy biennial herb used to flavor or garnish foods. There are several varieties.

Parsley Sauce: Butter sauce with chopped parsley. Served with fish.

Parsnip: An edible root vegetable; also used to flavor stock.

Paskha (Russ.): The traditional Russian Easter dessert, made with farmer's cheese, sour cream, butter, vanilla bean, sugar, nuts, raisins, and crystallized fruits, and moulded in a wooden form into a pyramid shape.

Passatelli (Ital.): Very thin egg noodles.

Pasta (Ital.): A wheat-flour product made in a multitude of different shapes — macaroni, spaghetti, noodles, etc.

Pasta Verde (Ital.): Pasta made with spinach as an ingredient — green noodles.

Paste: A mixture of flour and water, or a concentrated ground preparation such as anchovy or almond paste.

Pastiera di Grano (Ital.): Sweet Italian pie made with soaked wheat; traditional for Easter.

Pastina (Ital.): Tiny pasta, used in soups.

Pastrami: Highly spiced smoked beef, usually prepared from a shoulder cut.

Pastry: A stiff dough of flour, water, fat, etc., used for pie crust or patty shells. The various kinds of pastry include short pastry, pie pastry, puff or chou(x) pastry.

Pastry Bag: A cone-shaped bag used to pipe soft mixtures such as pastry dough or icing into decorative shapes.

Pastry Blender: A utensil used to cut fat into flour in making pastry.

Pastry Wheel: A small roller tool used to crimp the edges of a tart or other pastry.

Pâté (Fr.): A seasoned meat, liver, poultry, or fish paste that is baked and served hot or cold as a spread.

Pâte Brisée (Fr.): Butter-based pastry dough, used particularly for quiches.

Pâté de Compagne (Fr.): Country pâté made with rather coarsely ground ingredients — similar to the American meat loaf.

Pâté de Foie Gras (Fr.): A fine paste made from foie gras (q.v.), Madeira, and truffles.

Patty Shell: A shell made from puff paste to hold creamed mixtures or fruit.

Paupiettes (Fr.): Thin slices of meat rolled around a filling or stuffing.

Peach Melba: A dessert of vanilla ice cream, sliced peaches, and raspberry puree.

Peanut: A plant native to the United States producing a shelled nut that matures in the ground; the nut is eaten raw or made into butter or oil.

Pears Helène: Pears poached in vanilla syrup and served with ice cream and hot chocolate sauce.

Pecorino (Ital.): A strong, salted cheese with a characteristic aroma; made from sheep's milk.

Pectin: A white substance found in certain fruits and vegetables; used to make jellies.

Peel: The outer skin of certain fruits and vegetables.

Peking Duck: A Chinese dish of crisp roasted duck with meat and skin cut into squares. It is served in a light, crêpelike "doily" with sweet sauce and scallions.

Pekoe: A variety of tea.

Peperoni (Ital.): Green peppers or red sweet peppers; also, a spicy sausage.

Pepitas (Sp.): Dried, roasted pumpkin seeds.

Pepper: A spicy seasoning made from peppercorns. It can be used whole, coarsely or finely ground, or cracked. There are two kinds of pepper available — white and black. The black is the stronger.

Peppercorn: The whole pepper berry, before it is ground. See above.

Pepper Mill: A utensil for grinding whole peppercorns.

Pepperpot: A highly spiced stew with relatively little sauce.

Periwinkle: A small sea snail, eaten raw with a cocktail sauce.

Perrier Water: A bottled French natural mineral water.

Persillade (Fr.): Chopped parsley mixed with varying quantities of chopped garlic, sprinkled over cooked food.

Persimmon: A soft, sweet fruit of Japanese origin. It turns from yellow to bright orange-red as it ripens.

Pesce (Ital.): Fish.

Pestle: See Mortar and Pestle.

Pesto (Ital.): A thin paste made from crumbled basil leaves, garlic, sharp cheese, olive oil, and pine nuts (or walnuts). Served with pasta.

Petit Four (Fr.): Small, rich, decoratively iced cake.

Petit Marmite (Fr.): A strong, clear consommé cooked and served in an earthenware vessel; also, the vessel itself.

Petit-Suisse (Fr.): A very creamy, unsalted French cheese of the double-cream type, small and cylindrical in shape.

Petits Pois (Fr.): Green peas.

Phyllo Pastry: See Filo Pastry.

Piccalilli: A condiment consisting of cucumbers, green peppers, and onions pickled in vinegar, with mustard and spices.

Pickle: To preserve in brine or vinegar; also, the product of this process.

Pignoli (Ital.): Pine nuts.

Pilaf or Pilau: A rice dish, popular in Greece, the Near East, and Asia, that is flavored with saffron or turmeric and often contains meat, poultry, or fish.

Pimiento: Sweet red pepper used as a relish or as an ingredient in salads or coleslaw.

37

Pinch: An amount less than one-eighth of a teaspoon; as much as can be taken up between the thumb and index finger.

Pipe: To decorate with a mixture forced through the nozzle of a pastry tube.

Piquant: Sharp-flavored.

Piroshki (Russ.): Small baked tarts filled with meat, fish, rice, eggs, and/or cabbage.

Pissaladière (Fr.): A kind of tart made with onions, anchovy fillets, and black olives; somewhat similar to a pizza.

Pistou (Fr.): Pesto (q.v.).

Pit: To remove stones or pits from cherries or other stoned fruit.

Pita (Gr.): A round, flat bread with a pocket in which various stuffings are placed.

Pizza (Ital.): The generic term for any flat, baked pastry topped with tomato sauce, cheese, sausage, mushrooms, olives, et al.

Plaice: A saltwater fish, also known as flounder or fluke.

Plank: An oiled piece of oak, one inch thick, on which meat or fish is served, surrounded by cooked vegetables.

Plantain: A tropical plant related to the banana; also, the fruit of this plant, a staple food in the tropics.

Plattar (Swed.): A small, thin pancake baked in a special skillet containing shallow, round indentations.

Plombières (Fr.): A sweet, frozen, custard dessert.

Pluck: To remove the feathers of a bird after it has been killed.

Plump: To soak in water until soft and swollen, as dried fruit.

Poach: To simmer in liquid just below boiling point, 205°-210° F.

Poi: A Hawaiian food made from cooked taro root pounded to a paste and fermented.

Poire (Fr.): Pear.

Poireau (Fr.): Leek.

Poisson (Fr.): Fish.

Poivrade (Fr.) A peppery brown sauce used on meats and game.

Poivre (Fr.): Pepper.

Pojarski (Russ.): Oval cutlets of ground chicken or veal, crisp-fried and served in a creamy mushroom sauce.

Polenta (Ital.): Italian cornmeal mush, eaten hot, or chilled and sliced.

Pollo (Ital., Sp.): Chicken.

Polonaise, à la (Fr.): Garnished with hard-cooked, sieved egg yolk, butter, and crumbs.

Polpette (Ital.): Meatballs.

Polpettone (Ital.): Meat loaf.

Polyunsaturated: Denoting a class of fats of animal or vegetable origin, especially plant oils whose molecules consist of carbon chains with many double bands unsaturated by hydrogen atoms.

Pomegranate: A semitropical tree whose fruit is used to make grenadine syrup; also used as a flavoring in many fruit dishes.

Pomme (Fr.): Apple.

Pomme de Terre (Fr.): Potato.

Pomodoro (Ital.): Tomato.

Pompano: A South Atlantic and Gulf Coast fish.

Ponce Creole: Meat-and-yam-stuffed pig stomach; like a large sausage.

Pone: Flat, round cake, as corn pone.

Pont l'Evêque (Fr.): A semihard, fermented French cheese, made from whole or skimmed milk.

Popover: The American equivalent of Yorkshire pudding. A very light, puffy, hollow muffin, made with eggs, flour, and milk.

Poppy Seed: The seeds of the poppy, used in breads, cakes, and cookies, or for the extraction of poppy seed oil.

Porter: A dark, sweet beer; in England, strong and almost black.

Port-Salut (Fr.): Mild, semisoft table cheese with a nutty flavor.

Portugaise (Fr.): Portuguese-style; usually containing tomato in some form.

Potage (Fr.): A thick soup.

Potage St.-Germain (Fr.): A thick green-pea soup.

Potatoes Anna: Potatoes cut in thin, round slices, layered, and cooked in butter in a covered terrine or casserole no more than two inches deep.

Potato Masher: An implement used to mash boiled or baked potatoes.

Potato Starch: Flour made from potatoes, used as a thickening agent.

Pot, au (Fr.): Generally applied to meat or chicken cooked in a large pot with water or broth.

Pot-au-Feu (Fr.): Literally, "pot on the fire" — a rich beef-and-vegetable stew or soup.

Pot Roasting: A method of slow cooking by steam in a covered pan.

Pots au Crème (Fr.): Small, individual dishes containing a rich, mousselike pudding; usually served well chilled.

Potted: Term describing any food preserved in a jar.

Poule-au-Pot (Fr.): A pot-au-feu (q.v.) including a stuffed chicken.

Poulet (Fr.): Chicken.

Poulette Sauce: Allemande sauce (q.v.) to which lemon juice and parsley are added.

Pound: To beat or grind with a heavy implement, such as a meat mallet or a pestle.

Powdered Sugar: A finer grind than granulated, but in which the individual granules are still discernible.

Prairie Chicken: A grouselike game bird.

Praline: A crisp confection made of pecans in sugar syrup that is boiled until brown.

Prawn: A small crustacean of the shrimp family.

Precook: To cook food partially or completely before final cooking or reheating.

Preheat: To heat an oven to a required temperature before baking food.

Pretzel: A strip of dough tied in a loose knot, sprinkled with salt, and baked.

Prick: To pierce the surface of food with a fork or the point of a knife.

Prickly Pear: A cactus with an edible fruit that can be eaten raw or cooked into a stewlike mixture.

Printanière, à la (Fr.): Served or garnished with tender spring vegetables.

Process: In canning, to boil jars of food in a water bath or steam-pressure canner long enough to destroy microorganisms that cause spoilage.

Profiteroles (Fr.): Tiny cream puffs filled with sweet or savory mixtures.

Proof: To test yeast to see if it is alive and active.

Prosciutto (Ital.): Sweet, pale red ham cured and aged Italian-style. Served in paper-thin slices, usually with melon, as an appetizer; or used with cheese to fill boned veal or chicken breasts.

Provençale, à la (Fr.): Describes dishes originating in the region of France known as Provence and containing garlic, olive oil, and tomatoes.

Provolo (Ital.): A very mild smoked cheese.

Provolone (Ital.): A hard yellow cheese; the cheddar of southern Italy.

Pudding: A name given to numerous dishes, both sweet and savory, that are steamed, boiled, or baked.

Puffing: Refers to dehydrated foods such as raisins and mushrooms that are reconstituted in warm water, causing them to puff up before they are used.

Puff Paste or Pastry: A short, flaky pastry dough incorporating large amounts of butter, which puffs when baked and forms many thin layers.

Pulque (Sp.): Fermented sap of the century plant, used in making a Mexican liqueur.

Pumpernickel (Ger.): Dark, heavy-textured bread made from coarsely ground rye flour.

Puree: To press food through a fine sieve or food mill, or whirl in a blender to a smooth paste.

Purslane: Actually a weed, the leaves of which are used as a potherb and in salads.

Quail: Member of the partridge family; a small bird considered a delicacy when roasted.

Queen Olives: Olives grown strictly for eating.

Quenelle (Fr.): A dumpling made of ground fish or meat bound with eggs and poached in stock or water.

Queso (Sp.): A very creamy Mexican cheese.

Quiche (Fr.): A hot, savory custard tart made with cream, eggs, and cheese in a pastry shell. Of the many variations, Quiche Lorraine, made with bacon or ham, is perhaps the best known in this country.

Quince: A tart fruit with a high pectin content; used in making jam, jellies, marmalades, and syrups.

Rack: A rib section of meat; a roast containing several ribs.

Ragout: A rich brown stew containing meat and vegetables.

Rail Splitters: Corn-bread sticks.

Raisins: Dried sweet grapes.

Ramekin: A small oven-proof dish, used for both baking and serving individual portions.

Rasher: A slice of bacon or raw ham cut in varying thickness.

Raspings: Grated bread crusts.

Ratatouille (Fr.): A stew composed primarily of eggplant, zucchini, tomatoes, herbs, and spices.

Ravigote (Fr.): A cold sauce made of tarragon vinegar seasoned with chopped capers, finely chopped green onions, parsley, etc.; served on fish, seafood, and salads.

Ravioli (Ital.): Pasta squares with various fillings.

Reconstitute: To add water to concentrated food to return it to its natural form.

Red-Simmering: Chinese braising, or the slow simmering of meats, poultry, or game in soy sauce and other aromatics to produce a reddish color.

Red Snapper: Prized gourmet fish with a reddish skin.

Reduce: To boil down a liquid, reducing it in quantity and concentrating its flavor.

Refresh: To pour cold water over previously blanched and drained food.

Refritos (Sp.): Cooked, mashed, refried beans; a Mexican food.

Rehoboam: See table, "Oversize Wine Bottles," p. 61.

Religieuse (Fr.): A cake made with cream-filled, iced éclairs arranged in a pyramid and topped with a cream puff.

Relish: A highly flavored condiment usually consisting of pickles in some form. May also consist of different tart fruits, as apple-cranberry relish.

Relleño (Sp.): Chili pepper stuffed with meat, rice, and spicy seasonings.

Remoulade Sauce: A cold mayonnaise sauce flavored with mustard, anchovy paste, and chopped capers, parsley, gherkins, chervil, and tarragon.

Render: To free fat from connective tissue by heating slowly until the fat melts and can be drained off.

Rennet: A substance prepared from the inner lining of a calf or pig stomach and used to curdle or coagulate milk.

Rib: One branch of a bunch of celery; also referred to as a stalk.

Ricciolini (Ital.): Little curls of pasta.

Rice: To force food, such as boiled potatoes, through a fine sieve or ricer to give a light, fluffy consistency similar to rice.

Rice Vinegar: A mild, white vinegar; used in Chinese cookery.

Richelieu (Fr.): A garnish consisting of stuffed tomatoes, mushrooms, artichoke hearts, braised lettuce, and potatoes.

Ricotta (Ital.): A creamy Italian pot cheese, similar to cottage cheese.

Rigatoni (Ital.): A short, slightly curved, ridged macaroni tube.

Rijsttafel (Du.): Literally, "rice table" — a dinner of rice with many side dishes of meat, fish, vegetables, chicken, eggs, and sundry sauces.

Rinse: To place in a strainer or colander under running water for a few minutes and drain before using.

Ris de Veau (Fr.): Veal sweetbreads.

Risotto (Ital.): Rice cooked with broth and flavored with grated Italian cheese, saffron, and other seasonings.

Rissoles (Fr.): Meat-filled turnovers of puff pastry fried in deep fat or baked.

Roasting: A method of cooking meat, poultry, game, and fish on an open spit or in an oven so as to preserve the internal juices.

Robert Sauce: Brown sauce with onions, white wine, and mustard.

Rock Cornish Hens: Small birds weighing between one and one and a half pounds each; crossbred from Cornish Game and Plymouth Rock fowl.

Roe: Fish eggs.

Rollmops: Herring fillets marinated in seasoned wine, then rolled around a gherkin.

Roll Out: To roll dough into a thin, flat sheet with a rolling pin.

Roll Up: To roll a sheet of dough lengthwise, usually over a filling, jelly-roll fashion.

Romano (Ital.): A hard, white grating cheese with a tangy flavor.

Roquefort (Fr.): A piquant, white cheese made from sheep's milk and veined with a mottled blue mold.

Rosemary: The leaves of the perennial evergreen herb, used fresh or dried as seasoning.

Rotelle (Ital.): A type of pasta shaped like a small wheel.

Rôtie (Fr.): Toasted bread; also, generally — rôti or rôtie — roasted.

Roulades (Fr.): Like paupiettes (q.v.), thin slices of meat or fish strips rolled round a stuffing.

Roux (Fr.): A cooked paste of flour and butter or drippings, used as the basis of many sauces.

Royale (Fr.): A moulded egg custard used to garnish soups.

Rubber Ring: In canning, a flat rubber band used as a gasket between a metal or glass lid and the jar.

Rusk: Twice-roasted bread or a semi-sweet cake.

Russe, à la (Fr.): Russian-style.

Rye: Cereal grain, used in making flour, whiskey, and bread.

Sabayon (Fr.): A frothy dessert made of egg yolks beaten with sugar and Marsala wine. In Italy it is called zabaglione.

Saccharine: Commercial name for a sweet-tasting, water-soluble, crystalline chemical substance; used as a sugar substitute.

Sacher Torte (Ger.): A rich chocolate cake of Viennese origin, with apricot filling and dark chocolate icing.

Saddle: A cut of meat including the entire center section of the animal; that is, both loins.

Safflower: A thistlelike plant cultivated for the orange dye from its flower and the oil from its seed.

Saffron: A very expensive, powdered spice made from the dried orange-colored stigmas of the autumn crocus. It is used sparingly in recipes to add color and a very distinctive taste; essential to bouillabaisse (q.v.).

Sage: A herb used to flavor marinades, poultry stuffings, forcemeats, and green vegetables. Can also refer to a cheddarlike cheese flavored with the dried herb.

Sago: A floury extract of the marrow of various kinds of palm trees, used in cooking and baking as a liaison. Also, a cheese.

St.-Honoré (Fr.): An elegant and fancy cake with a cream filling, surrounded by a ring of small, sugar-glazed cream puffs.

Saki (Jap.): A fermented rice wine, usually served warm.

Salami (Ital.): A highly spiced, salty sausage, either hard or soft in consistency, that originated in Italy.

Salmagundi: An ancient English dish made of chopped meats, hard-boiled eggs, beets, and pickles.

Salmanazar: See table, "Oversize Wine Bottles," p. 61.

Salpicon (Fr.): One or more ingredients diced small and bound with sauce, hot or cold, white or brown.

Salsa (Ital. or Sp.): Sauce; also a specific and highly spiced table sauce.

Salsa de Chile Guero (Sp.): A Mexican sauce of cooked green chilies.

Salsa Tounata (Ital.): A sauce made with tuna fish.

Salsify: A white, fleshy root vegetable with an oysterlike flavor; also called oyster plant.

Salt: To treat fish, meat, or other substances with salt, or to immerse in a preserving brine.

Saltimbocca (Ital.): A classic Italian dish of veal and ham, whose name means literally "jump into your mouth"!

Saltpeter: Potassium nitrate, used with salt for pickling and preserving meat.

Salvia (Ital.): Sage (q.v.).

Sambals: Rice mixed with various cooked foods and a very spicy pepper sauce, usually served in the shape of a small pyramid.

Sangría (Sp.): A beverage made by mixing Madeira with fruit juice, water, sugar, and grated nutmeg.

Sapsago: A hard, cone-shaped Swiss cheese filled with finely ground aromatic cloves. It has a pungent flavor and is usually used only for grating.

Sardellen (Ger.): Anchovies.

Sardines: Small fish from Sardinia, usually canned and preserved in olive oil, but also eaten fresh.

Sardo (Ital.): A hard, pungent, and salty cheese from Sardinia.

Sargasso: Name of a seaweed used in Spain as a salad ingredient.

Sarsaparilla: Flavoring obtained from smilax roots and used in beverages.

Sashimi (Jap.): A fish sliced paper-thin and served raw.

Sassafras: An infusion of the bark and leaves of a tree of the laurel family. Used as a tea or to flavor other beverages (such as root beer).

Sauce: Liquid accompaniment to food that enhances or alters its flavor.

Sauerbraten (Ger.): Pot roast of beef marinated in a spiced vinegar mixture, then braised on top of the stove or in the oven.

Sauerkraut (Ger.): Finely shredded cabbage fermented in brine.

Sauté (Fr.): To cook in a small amount of fat, oil, or butter.

Savarin (Fr.): French version of baba (q.v.) — cake soaked in rum or kirsch.

Savory (or Savoury): British term for food served after dessert and before coffee. Cheese straws, canapés, deviled chicken wings, and Welsh rarebit are all typical savories. Also a herb. See Summer Savory.

Scald: To heat milk or other liquid to below the boiling point, about 200° F. Milk is scalded when tiny bubbles appear around the edges of the pan.

42

Scale: To strip the scales from a fish.

Scallions: Also called green or spring onions; the American equivalent of young leeks.

Scallop: To bake in a cream sauce topped with crumbs; also, a shellfish.

Scallopini (Ital.): Small, thin pieces of meat, usually veal.

Scampi (Ital.): Shrimp; also, a shrimp dish cooked in a garlic sauce.

Schnecken (Ger.): Sweet buns made of coiled yeast dough and topped with cinnamon, walnuts, and sugar; "snails."

Schnitzel (Ger.): A thin cutlet of veal fried lightly in butter.

Scones: Round or square baking-soda biscuits, served with butter and jam. A favorite in Scotland, England, and Ireland.

Score: To gash meat in order to prevent curling during cooking.

Scotch Eggs: Hard-boiled eggs encased in sausage meat, rolled in cracker crumbs, and deep-fried.

Scotch Woodcock: Scrambled egg-yolk-and-cream mixture poured over anchovy (q.v.) toast.

Scrape: To remove the outer skin of vegetables by scraping with the blade of a paring knife or vegetable peeler, as carrots.

Seafood: A general term for crustaceans and shellfish.

Sear: To expose the surface of a food, usually meat, to a very high temperature for a short time, in either a hot oven or a skillet, to seal in the juices.

Sea Salt or Coarse Salt: Also referred to as Bay Salt; made by evaporating sea water. Kosher salt is a coarse-grained sea salt.

Season: To add salt, pepper, or other seasonings to food.

Sediment: A deposit found in the bottom of wine bottles.

Seed: To remove seeds from vegetables such as tomatoes, peppers, or cucumbers.

Self-Rising Flour: Flour containing a rising agent mixed in during manufacture.

Semolina: Large wheat grains left after the flour is milled; principally used for making macaroni products.

Senegalese: A rich, creamy soup with a chicken-stock base, served cold with or without curry and bits of chicken.

Separate: To separate the white of an egg from the yolk.

Serrate: To cut a decorative, notched border into food or pastries.

Serviette, à la (Fr.): Describes food served in a folded napkin.

Sesame Oil: A highly aromatic flavoring made from toasted sesame seeds, used primarily in Oriental cookery.

Sesame Paste: An aromatic, strongly flavored seasoning, prepared from finely ground, toasted sesame seeds.

Sesame Seed: The seed of an annual tropical herbaceous plant used in baking and candy-making; also called benne.

Set: Firm enough to hold its shape; usually applied to gelatin or jellied dishes.

Setting Time: A period of carry-over cooking occurring when food is removed hot from the oven and allowed to stand.

Seven Spice Red Pepper: A hot blend of peppers and other spices, used in Oriental cookery.

Seviche (Sp.): Pickled raw fish served as an appetizer.

Shad: A sea fish related to the herring, which spawns in rivers and whose roe is considered a delicacy.

Shallots: Small bulbs of the onion *(Allium)* family, having a mild, garlic-like taste.

Shark's Fin: An important dish at most Chinese banquets, prepared from the chewy, cartilaginous back- or tail-fin of the fish.

Shashlik (Russ.): Cubes of young lamb, marinated, skewered, and broiled. See also Kebab and Shish Kebab.

43

Shepherd's Pie: A traditional English meat-and-potato pot pie.

Sherbet: A fruit ice made with milk or egg white.

Shirr: To bake whole eggs with cream or crumbs in a buttered ramekin.

Shish Kebab: Meat cubes broiled on a skewer, often with vegetables. See also Kebab and Shashlik.

Shitake (Jap.): Brown or tan mushrooms, usually dried and reconstituted.

Shortbread: A rich cookie made of flour, sugar, and butter.

Shortening: Refers to the various kinds of fat used in baking and cooking; in America, often more particularly solid vegetable shortening.

Shred: To cut with a very sharp knife or special shredder into thin, narrow strips.

Shuck: To remove the shells from shellfish, such as clams or oysters; also, to remove husks from corn.

Sieve: A bowl-shaped wire screen used to drain off liquids or to puree food.

Sift: To separate out coarse particles from dry ingredients, such as flour, by shaking through a sieve.

Simmer: To cook in liquid below boiling point, or at about 185° F. The liquid should do no more than move gently, with bubbles forming below the surface.

Singe: To burn off the down or hairs from plucked game or poultry with a flame, taking care not to char the skin.

Sirloin: A cut of beef, whole or divided, that can be roasted, braised, broiled, fried, or baked.

Skate: A large, flat, scaleless fish, prepared in many ways.

Skewer: A slim metal rod used to spear food to be grilled or broiled. Also denotes a small metal pin used to fasten foods together or to close the stuffed cavity of a turkey or chicken before cooking.

Skim: To remove fat or other floating matter from the surface of a liquid with a spoon or skimmer.

Skimmer: A flat, perforated utensil used for skimming.

Sling: A cold drink, usually made with cracked ice, sugar, an alcoholic liquor, and flavorings.

Sliver: To cut into small, thin, and narrow pieces.

Smelt: A small, delicately fleshed, freshwater fish.

Smetana (Russ.): Sour cream.

Smoke: To preserve meat or fish by exposure to the aromatic smoke of burning hardwood, usually after pickling in brine.

Smorgasbord: A meal featuring a varied number of hot or cold dishes served buffet style.

Smørrebrød (Dan.): Elaborate, open-faced sandwiches.

Snail: A small mollusk, usually taken from its shell, boiled or steamed, then replaced in the shell and served with garlic butter. For the average American cook, this is a rather tedious process; but snails can be purchased already cooked and in the shell — expensive, but perhaps justly so in view of the time involved. A delicacy.

Snip: To cut in fine pieces with scissors, as chives.

Snow Peas: The pods of the sugar pea, picked and cooked before peas have formed within the pods. Also known as pea pods or Chinese peas.

Soak: To let food sit in liquid until thoroughly moistened, or swelled, as dried legumes.

Sodium Benzoate: Food preservative.

Soft-Ball Stage: Candy-making term. When a little hot sugar syrup dropped into cold water forms a ball that collapses when removed from the water, the temperature of the boiling sugar syrup is 234°-240° F.

Soft-Crack Stage: Candy-making term. When a little hot sugar syrup dropped into cold water separates into firm, but not brittle threads, the temperature of the boiling syrup is 270°-290° F.

Soft Peaks: Term used to describe a stage in beating egg whites when the egg whites are beaten enough so that the tips of the peak or peaks left from lifting the beater fold or curl over, being not quite stiff enough to hold their entire shape.

Sole: A flat, oval fish with firm, white flesh easily detached from the bone. True sole does not live in North American waters, but lemon sole or flounder is often substituted for true sole.

Sommelier (Fr.): A restaurant employee charged with the care and serving of wine.

Sorbet (Fr.): Sherbet (q.v.).

Sorrel: A hardy perennial herb, whose young tender leaves are used in salad; also used to flavor soups and sauces.

Soubise Sauce: Basically a puree of onions mixed with béchamel sauce and lightly flavored with nutmeg; served with meat or eggs.

Soufflé (Fr): A baked or chilled main dish or dessert made light and fluffy by the incorporation of stiffly beaten egg whites (if baked) or whipped cream (if chilled).

Soya: A Chinese cheese made from the fermented juice of the soybean.

Soybean Sprouts: The sprouts of yellow soybeans.

Soy Sauce: A thin, brown, and very salty sauce, used extensively in Oriental cooking. Adds color and flavor to marinades.

Spaetzle (Ger.): Tiny dumplings.

Spaghetti (Ital.): Literally, "strings." Long, thin rods of pasta of different sizes, including capellini (very, very fine), fedelini (very fine), spaghettini (thin), spaghetti (medium), and spaghettoni (large).

Spanakopita (Gr.): Spinach or cheese pie made with flaky filo (phyllo) pastry.

Spanish Olives: Green olives stuffed with pimiento; an appetizer.

Spatula: A flat blade of wood, metal, or rubber, used to spread soft mixtures evenly.

Spice: To add seasonings or condiments to impart flavor; also, a substance that imparts flavor.

Spiedini (Ital.): Skewered meat rolls and cheese dipped in egg and crumbs, fried, and served on a bed of noodles.

Spit: A thin, pointed metal rod used to hold and turn roasting meats or poultry over a fire.

Spoilage: Deterioration or decay, making food unfit or unsafe to eat. Indications of spoilage in canned food include a bulging cap or lid, an unnatural odor, an uncharacteristic appearance, a sour taste, or a cloudy liquid.

Sponge: A frothy gelatin dessert; also, a mixture of flour and yeast allowed to rise and used to leaven bread.

Sprat: A small fish, usually dried; a Scandinavian favorite.

Springerle (Ger.): Decoratively moulded, anise-flavored cookies; traditional for Christmas.

Spumante (Ital.): A term denoting a sparkling wine.

Spumoni (Ital.): Light, creamy ice cream, made with egg white or whipped cream, variously flavored and colored.

Spun Sugar: Sugar syrup boiled until it forms threads, then whirled.

Squabs: Young domestic pigeons, cooked and served like Rock Cornish hens.

Standing Time: The time cooked food should stand or "rest" before being served.

Star Anise: A dried, star-shaped spice, used in Oriental cooking and a substitute for bay leaf.

Starch: A thickening agent contained in rice, corn, wheat, potatoes, or arrowroot.

Steam: To cook in a covered pot over or in a small amount of boiling water.

Steel: A tool used to sharpen knives.

Steep: To place food in water below the

boiling point in order to extract color or flavor.

Sterilize: To destroy microorganisms by boiling, or subjecting to dry heat or steam.

Stew: To cook in liquid to cover at a low to moderate temperature; also, food so cooked.

Stiff Peaks: Term used to describe egg whites beaten to the point that when the beater is lifted, the peaks stand up straight and keep their shape, but are still moist and glossy.

Stilton: A rich, waxy English cheese veined with blue-green mold.

Stir: To blend without beating by mixing with a spoon in a circular motion.

Stir Fry: A quick-frying technique, used primarily in the preparation of Chinese food.

Stock: The liquor or broth obtained by cooking meat, fish, fowl, or vegetables in water. See also Broth.

Stollen (Ger.): Large, fruited yeast breads, traditional at Christmas.

Strain: To drain liquid from solid food; to puree by rubbing through a sieve.

Strudel (Ger.): Thin, flaky pastry, layered or stuffed with a variety of fillings, such as apple, nut, cheese, meat, etc.

Stud: To force flavoring or garnish into the surface of food, as a ham studded with cloves.

Stuff: To fill one food with another.

Stuffing: A seasoned filling.

Sub Gum (Chin.): A vegetable stew.

Subric (Fr.): A small, uncoated croquette.

Suet: The hard, fatty tissue surrounding the kidneys of animals, often rendered to liquid fat.

Sukiyaki (Jap.): A dish of meat, vegetables, and seasonings, usually cooked at the table.

Summer Savory: Garden herb with a thymelike flavor.

Sunflower Oil: A cooking oil prepared from sunflower seeds.

Suprême (Fr.): A boned chicken breast.

Supreme Sauce: A smooth white sauce like velouté (q.v.), made with chicken stock and thick cream.

Sushi (Jap.): Moulded, vinegared rice combined with a variety of other ingredients and topped with raw seafood.

Sweat: To draw out flavor by cooking diced vegetables gently in a covered pan with a little melted butter until soft but not browned.

Sweetbreads: The thymus gland of a calf. A delicacy that may be prepared in many ways.

Swirl: To rotate liquid in a pan to loosen clinging particles of cooked food.

Sword Bean: A type of edible broad bean.

Syllabub: A frothy milk punch.

Syrup: Sugar combined with water or fruit juice and boiled to a smooth and sticky liquid; used hot or cold.

Tabasco: The trade name for a pungent, red-pepper sauce.

Table d'Hôte (Fr.): A meal of several specific courses offered in a restaurant at a set, overall price.

Taboule (or Tabooli): A Middle-Eastern salad made of cracked wheat, tomatoes, onions, parsley, olive oil, and salt.

Taco (Sp.): A tortilla wrapped or folded around a filling; may be crisp or soft.

Tagliatelle (Ital.): Wide-cut noodles.

Tagliolini (Ital.): Thin noodles of the tagliatelle family, used in broth.

Tahina: Oily paste of crushed sesame seeds and chickpeas, used in Middle-Eastern cooking.

Tamale: A chili-seasoned cornmeal dough mixture; filled, rolled, and wrapped in a cornhusk, then steamed.

Tamara (Ital.): An Italian mixed spice, usually containing cinnamon and fennel.

Tamari: A kind of soy sauce that has been fermented, used in seasoning soups, salads, and casseroles.

Tamarind: Fruit of the tamarind tree; the acid, juicy pulp is used in lemonade.

Tarama (Gr.): The red roe of carp or mullet.

Taro: A tropical plant with a starchy, edible rootstock; baked and ground, it is made into a paste, which is then fermented to become poi, a food staple of Hawaii.

Tarragon: A potherb used in sauces, or to flavor eggs, salads, chicken, or vinegar.

Tartar Sauce: Mayonnaise mixed with chopped hard-boiled egg, mustard, and chopped pickle; served primarily with fish.

Tavel: A rosé wine.

Tea Caddy: A container for loose tea leaves.

Tempura (Jap.): Batter-dipped, fried seafood or vegetables.

Tenderize: To break down tough connective tissue in meat by marinating, pounding with a meat mallet, or sprinkling with a commercial meat tenderizer.

Tequila (Sp.): A Mexican liquor distilled from the century plant.

Terrapin: A land turtle.

Terrine (Fr.): A loaf of diced, ground, shredded, or minced meat, poultry, or liver, cooked in an earthenware container and served cold, as pâté; also, the term for the container itself.

Thicken: To add flour, cornstarch, egg yolk, or other thickening agent to a liquid mixture.

Thin: To dilute a mixture with a liquid.

Thyme: A herb with small, grey-green leaves and a pleasant odor, used to flavor stews, salads, and soups.

Tilsit (Ger.): A mild cheese of the port-salut (q.v.) type.

Timbale (Fr.): A round pastry casing for various fillings; also, the metal mould in which the pastry is baked.

Tipsy Cake: Sponge cake made with sherry and stewed fruit, topped with custard and cream.

Tiropita (Gr.): A puffy cheese pie made with filo (phyllo) pastry (q.v.), feta cheese, and eggs.

Toad-in-the-Hole: An English dish of sausage baked in batter as a kind of puffy pudding; also, a fried egg cooked in a hole in the center of a piece of bread.

Toast: To brown bread by direct heat or in an oven.

Toast Points: Slices of toast cut in half diagonally with the crusts removed; served with or under food.

Tofu (Chin.): Bean curd and bean cakes; smooth, bland, creamy custard made of pureed soybeans pressed into cakes.

Tokay: A Hungarian wine; also, the grape from which it is made.

Tomalley: The liver of a lobster, greenish when cooked. Considered a delicacy.

Tomato Coulis: A mixture of strong tomato puree and sliced, whole, skinned tomatoes, cooked in butter and flavored with garlic.

Tomato Paste: A thick, concentrated paste made of tomatoes; used to enrich and thicken tomato or other sauces.

Tomato Puree: A thick combination of coarsely chopped tomatoes and spices. Not as concentrated as tomato paste but used in much the same way.

Tomato Sauce: Made from tomatoes, olive oil, onion, herbs, and often meat, stocks, cooked together. The traditional sauce for spaghetti.

Torrone (Ital.): Italian nougat-type candy, made of egg whites, sugar, and almonds.

Torte (Ger.): Any extremely light, delicate cake baked in round layers and filled with whipped cream, fruit, chocolate, jams, and jellies.

Tortelli (Ital.): Raviolilike dumplings stuffed with greens and ricotta cheese.

Tortellini (Ital.): Small, ring-shaped dumplings usually stuffed with a meat filling.

Tortelloni (Ital.): Large, square dumplings usually stuffed with Swiss chard or spinach.

Tortilla (Sp.): Flat, thin Mexican corn or flour cake; also refers to an omelet.

Toss: To mix with light strokes, lifting with a fork and spoon and flipping in the air, as salads.

Tournedos (Fr.): The choicest slices from the finest fillet of beef, cut thick and round.

Transparent Noodles: A kind of slender, somewhat gelatinous vermicelli.

Treacle: British molasses.

Tree Ears: A form of fungus that grows on trees and is a good source of protein. Gives an interesting gelatinous texture to other foods. Used in Chinese cooking.

Trifle: A puddinglike dessert made of coarsely crumbled cake, whiskey, fruit, and whipped cream.

Trim: To cut away unwanted or unsightly parts of food before or after cooking; to shape.

Truffle: A rare, round, wrinkled black fungus, usually one or two inches in diameter, found underground around the bases of oak trees in certain regions of France and Italy. Considered a delicacy.

Truss: To tie the wings and legs of a bird to the body by means of skewers and string so that it keeps its shape during cooking.

Trussing Needle: A steel rod pointed at one end, pierced at the other end, and used to sew shut the body cavity of poultry before cooking.

Try Out: To render (q.v.).

Tsimmes or Tzimmes: A Jewish casserole of sweet potatoes, prunes, and carrots, made without meat.

Tufoli (Ital.): Large pasta tubes designed to be stuffed.

Tuna: Any one of various large marine and food fishes. The albacore, sometimes called "tunny," is the one most sold commercially as canned tuna.

Turban: Describes food arranged in a circle or cooked in a ring mould.

Turbot: Large, white-fleshed, flat fish, similar to halibut; also, in New England, any white fish cooked in a cream sauce.

Tureen: A large, deep container used primarily for serving soup.

Turmeric: An East-Indian plant whose aromatic rootstock is dried and used powdered as a spice for pickling or as an essential ingredient of curry powder.

Turn: To flip over or reverse food during the cooking process; also, to trim vegetables into small shapes for garnish.

Ugli (or Ugly) Fruit: A thick-skinned, globular fruit resembling grapefruit, with no marked flavor, but a pleasant odor and texture.

Unmould: To remove any kind of food from its container, especially ice cream or gelatin mixtures.

Vacherin (Fr.): An elaborate dessert with cream-filled meringues heaped on a sweet pastry base.

Valencia Orange: Spanish orange.

Valenciennes, à la (Fr.): A method of cooking chicken with rice.

Vanilla: The pod of a climbing plant native to Mexico, cultivated in various tropical regions, and widely used as a flavoring, either as the pod itself (vanilla bean), powdered, or, mainly in America, as vanilla extract.

Vapeur, à la (Fr.): Term used to describe foods that are steamed.

Velouté Sauce: A basic white sauce made with veal or chicken stock and used as a basis for other sauces.

Venting or Exhausting: Canning term. An initial step in the steam-pressure method of canning that permits air to escape for ten minutes through the open vent of the canner.

Verjuice: The juice of unripe fruits such as grapes, used as a vinegar substitute in acidulating water. See Acidulated Water.

Vermicelli (Ital.): "Little worms" — denoting a thin spaghetti available in straight or looped rods.

Vermouth: A sweet or dry apéritif white wine flavored with aromatic herbs and spices.

Veronikas: Crescent-shaped tarts of Jewish origin, made of noodle dough and filled with meat or berries.

Véronique (Fr.): Describes dishes using seedless green grapes and white wine, e.g., sole véronique.

Vert, au (Fr.): Served in or with a sauce colored green with dill, parsley, or spinach.

Verte Sauce: Mayonnaise mixed with a puree of blanched strained herbs; green mayonnaise.

Vert Pré, au (Fr.): Term used to describe grilled meats garnished with straw potatoes and watercress; also, foods coated with green mayonnaise or verte sauce (q.v.).

Viandes (Fr.): Meats.

Vichyssoise (Fr.): A creamy potato and leek soup usually served cold and garnished with chives.

Vinaigrette (Fr.): Term describing meats or vegetables marinated or sauced with a mixture of oil and vinegar seasoned with salt, pepper, and sometimes chopped herbs.

Vin Blanc (Fr.): White wine.

Vinegar: An impure dilute solution of acetic acid, obtained by fermentation of wine or cider beyond the alcoholic stage, and used as a condiment and preservative.

Vin Rouge (Fr.): Red wine.

Vol-au-Vent (Fr.): Puff pastry filled with creamed mixtures of chicken, sweetbreads, meat, or fish.

Waffle Iron: A special grill used to make waffles.

Water Chestnut: A small tuber generally resembling the Occidental chestnut, but more moist and crisp in texture.

Water Jacket: Shallow pan of hot water in which a mould or dish of food is set to bake.

Welsh Rabbit (or Rarebit): A dish consisting of melted cheese, cream or milk, and wine or beer, seasoned with spices, and served in a chafing dish or on toast points. May also be served as a fondue (q.v.) in a fondue pot.

Wheat Gluten: A commercially available, high protein food, sold in either fresh or dried form.

Whey: The liquid in milk that is drained from the curd in the making of cheese.

Whip: To beat rapidly with a whisk, beater, or mixer foods such as eggs, cream, or jelly, in order to incorporate air and produce expansion.

Whisk: A utensil used to beat or whip eggs, cream, and sauces.

49

Wiener Schnitzel (Ger.): A veal cutlet.

Wild Rice: A highly prized, long-grained brown rice, grown in small quantities and, therefore, expensive.

Wine Vinegar: Vinegar (q.v.) made from wine; used mainly in salad dressings.

Wintergreen: An aromatic wild plant whose leaves (or the oil obtained from them) are used to flavor candy and chewing gum.

Winter Melon: A large melon with white, delicate flesh; used for soup in Chinese cookery.

Wok (Chin.): A metal cooking pan that resembles a salad bowl with handles; comes in various sizes. Used for stir-frying.

Won Ton (Chin.): Chinese noodle similar to ravioli (q.v.), encasing a filling of meat, fish, or vegetables.

Work: To knead or mix slowly.

Wormwood: A bitter herb; formerly used in the manufacture of absinthe.

Wurst (Ger.): Sausage.

Yarrow: An aromatic herb; the leaves are used in omelets and salads.

Yeast: A leavening agent, available commercially in either dried or compressed form.

Yogurt or Yoghurt: A semisolid, creamy milk culture with a sour taste, used extensively in cooking or eaten by itself, with or without added flavoring.

Yorkshire Pudding: Popover (q.v.) batter baked in the drippings of roast beef.

Zabaglione (Ital.): See Sabayon.

Zest: The outer rind of citrus fruits.

Zester: An instrument used to peel off the outer rind of citrus fruits.

Ziti (Ital.): A narrow, straight, tubular pasta.

Zuppa Inglese (Ital.): Literally, "English Soup." An odd name for this delicate and very Italian layer cake filled with custard, sometimes with candied fruit, and soaked in rum.

Zwieback (Ger.): A kind of biscuit or rusk, commonly used by babies for teething, but with many culinary uses as well.

BAKING TIMES & TEMPERATURES

Cakes and Cookies

Cakes	Time (minutes)	Temperature
Angel	60	325° F.
Cakes made with shortening:		
Cupcakes	20 to 25	350° F.
Layers	25 to 30	375° F.
Loaf	45 to 60	350° F.
Sheet	15 to 30	375° F.
Fruit	2 to 4 hours	250° to 275° F.
Sponge	60	325° F.

Cookies	Time (minutes)	Temperature
Drop	10 to 15	400° F.
Molasses	10 to 15	350° F.
Pan	25 to 30	350° F.
Refrigerator	8 to 12	400° F.
Rolled	8 to 12	400° F.

Meat, Poultry, and Fish

Meat*	Time (minutes)	Temperature
Beef, rare	18 to 20 per pound	300° F.
Beef, medium	22 to 25 per pound	300° F.
Beef, well done	27 to 30 per pound	300° F.
Ham, smoked	30 per pound	300° F.
Lamb, pink	15 per pound	325° F.
Lamb, well done	30 per pound	300° F.
Pork	40 per pound	350° F.
Veal	30 per pound	325° F.
*All rolled roasts	Add 10 to 15 minutes per pound	

Poultry	Time (minutes)	Temperature
Chicken	25 per pound	350° F.
Duck	25 per pound	350° F.
Turkey, small	25 per pound	300° F.
Turkey, large	20 per pound	275° F.

Fish	Time (minutes)	Temperature
Fish	20 per pound	375° F.

Pastries and Puddings

Pastries	Time (minutes)	Temperature
Custard or pumpkin pie	35	400° F.
Meringue shell	10 to 15	350° F.
Pastry shell	12 to 15	450° F.
Two-crust with cooked filling	25 to 35	425° F.
Two-crust with uncooked filling	30 to 45	400° F.

Puddings	Time (minutes)	Temperature
Bread	40 to 50	350° F.
Custard	25 to 30	325° F.
Rice	60	300° F.

Yeast and Quick Breads

Yeast Breads	Time (minutes)	Temperature
Loaves	50 to 60	400° F.
Rolls	20 to 30	400° F.

Quick Breads	Time (minutes)	Temperature
Biscuits	12 to 15	450° F.
Corn Bread	25 to 30	400° F.
Gingerbread	30 to 40	325° F.
Muffins	20 to 25	400° F.
Nut Bread	50 to 60	350° F.
Popovers	30 to 40	425° F.

Oven Temperatures

Particularly useful when dealing with old recipes based on the use of a wood or coal stove.

Very Slow	250°-275° F.
Slow	300°-325° F.
Moderate	350°-375° F.
Hot	400°-425° F.
Very Hot	450°-475° F.
Extremely Hot, or Broil	500°-525° F.

Temperature Conversion

Fahrenheit to Celsius (centigrade): Subtract 32 from the Fahrenheit number, multiply by 5, and divide by 9. For example, to convert the Fahrenheit freezing point, 32° F., to the Celsius equivalent — subtract 32, and you have 0, times 5 equals 0, divided by 9 equals 0 again, or the Celsius freezing point of 0° C. Similarly, to convert the Fahrenheit boiling point, 212° F., to the Celsius equivalent — subtract 32, and you have 180, times 5 equals 900, divided by 9 equals 100, or the Celsius boiling point of 100° C.

Celsius (centigrade) to Fahrenheit: The process is just the reverse, i.e., multiply the Celsius number by 9, divide by 5, and add 32. For example, to convert an oven temperature given as 177° C. to the Fahrenheit equivalent — multiply by 9, and you have 1593, divided by 5 equals 318.6, plus 32 equals 350.6° F., or a moderate oven.

Measures & Measurements

Fractional Measures

Dash (liquid)	=	Few drops
Dash, pinch, or "few grains" (dry)	=	Less than ⅛ teaspoon
1½ teaspoons	=	½ tablespoon
2 tablespoons	=	⅛ cup or 1 ounce liquid
2 tablespoons plus 2 teaspoons	=	⅙ (half of ⅓) cup
¼ cup plus 2 tablespoons	=	Half of ¾ cup
10 tablespoons plus 2 teaspoons	=	⅔ cup
12 tablespoons	=	¾ cup

How to Measure Exactly

In the directions that follow, a "dry-measuring cup" means a measuring cup which contains exactly its measure (¼ cup, ½ cup, 1 cup, 1 pint, or 1 quart) when filled to the brim, so that the contents may then be leveled off with a knife or spatula. For liquids, a measuring cup may have its full measure marked a little below the rim.

Butter (or margarine): Measured in the same way as Solid Shortening (see below). If stick butter or margarine is used, the following equivalents are valid: ¼ stick = 2 tablespoons; ½ stick = 4 tablespoons or ¼ cup; 1 stick = ½ cup or ¼ pound; 2 sticks = 1 cup or ½ pound; and 4 sticks = 2 cups or 1 pound.

Grated Cheese: Pack lightly into a dry-measuring cup until level with top.

Fat: May be measured either solid or melted, in any measuring cup. Fat is easier to measure melted, but the end amount will be the same, melted or solid. Measure solid fat as you would Solid Shortening (see below), melted fat or salad oil as you would any liquid.

Flour: Spoon lightly into a dry-measuring cup to overflowing and level off. Most all-purpose or enriched flours today are presifted and need no further sifting (the package will state "needs no sifting" or "presifted"). Otherwise, flours should be sifted before being measured. Cake flours usually need sifting.

Dried Fruit: Pack lightly into a dry-measuring cup until level with the top or the measurement required.

Milk (or other liquid): Place any measuring cup on level surface. Pour liquid into cup to desired level.

Molasses (or other syrup): Grease the measuring cup lightly before pouring in the syrup — thus, no molasses or other syrup will adhere to the walls of the cup when poured out, and you will get a fuller measure. If you have a dry-measuring cup for the exact measure required, so much the better, as the molasses will mound and should be leveled with a spatula or knife, as for any dry measure. Remove the syrup from the cup with a rubber spatula.

Solid Shortening: If less than ¼ cup is required, use a measuring spoon, packing in the shortening firmly. For measurements of any fraction of a 1-cup or other size measuring cup, use the water-replacement method, as follows: subtract the amount of shortening called for in the recipe from the total volume of the measuring cup (for example, ⅔ cup of shortening is required, so 1 cup minus ⅔ cup equals ⅓ cup); put the resulting amount (in the example, ⅓ cup) of cold water in the cup. Then add solid shortening until the water in the cup reaches the 1-cup level, and the shortening added is completely covered with water. Drain off the water, and remove the shortening with a rubber spatula. The amount will be exactly ⅔ cup. For measurements equaling the volume of a particular measuring cup or utensil, follow the same procedure as with measuring spoons; i.e., pack shortening in solidly, and scoop out of cup with a rubber spatula.

Spices, Salt, Baking Powder and Soda, and Cream of Tartar: Fill measuring spoon to overflowing and level off.

Sugar:

Brown Sugar — If dry, hard, or lumpy, should be pulverized in an electric blender or with a rolling pin before measuring. Unless a recipe specifically states otherwise, brown sugar should be firmly packed into a dry-measuring cup and leveled off. It should hold its shape when turned

out of the measuring cup. (To minimize hardening or lumping, refrigerate opened packages of brown sugar.) *Confectioners' Sugar* — Sift before measuring. Spoon sifted sugar lightly into a dry-measuring cup and level off.
Granulated Sugar — Sift only if lumpy. Spoon lightly into a dry-measuring cup and level off.

Metric Measures and Equivalents

Liquid Measure

The basic metric unit of liquid measure is the liter, equal to 1.06 quarts. A milliliter is one thousandth of a liter; a centiliter is one hundredth of a liter; a deciliter is one tenth of a liter; and a kiloliter is one thousand liters.

10 milliliters	=	1 centiliter
10 centiliters	=	1 deciliter
10 deciliters	=	1 liter
1000 liters	=	1 kiloliter

Equivalents

5 milliliters	=	1 teaspoon
15 milliliters	=	1 tablespoon
12 centiliters	=	½ cup
.24 liter	=	1 cup
.47 liter	=	1 pint
.95 liter	=	1 quart
3.79 liters	=	1 gallon

Weight Measure

The basic metric unit of weight measure is the gram, equal to one twenty-eighth of an ounce. A microgram is one millionth of a gram; a milligram is one thousandth of a gram; a centigram is one hundredth of a gram; and a kilogram is one thousand grams.

1000 micrograms	=	1 milligram
1000 milligrams	=	1 centigram
100 centigrams	=	1 gram
1000 grams	=	1 kilogram

Equivalents

1 gram	=	.035 ounce
28 grams	=	1 ounce
100 grams	=	3.5 ounces
227 grams	=	8 ounces
454 grams	=	1 pound
500 grams	=	1 pound, 1½ ounces (17.5 ounces)
1 kilogram	=	2.2 pounds

What Equals What

Liquid Measure

Used in American recipes for flour, sugar, shortening, diced fruits and vegetables, meat, et al., as well as for liquids.

This Measurement		Equals This
3 teaspoons	=	1 tablespoon
2 tablespoons	=	⅛ cup or 1 ounce liquid
4 tablespoons	=	¼ cup or 2 ounces liquid
6 tablespoons	=	⅜ cup or 3 ounces liquid
7 tablespoons	=	⅓ cup
8 tablespoons or 1 gill	=	½ cup, 1 "teacup," or 4 ounces liquid
16 tablespoons	=	1 cup
1 cup	=	½ pint or 8 ounces
2 cups	=	1 pint
4 cups	=	1 quart
2 pints	=	1 quart
4 quarts	=	1 gallon

Dry Measure

Dry measure pints and quarts, as berries, for example, are about ⅙ larger than their liquid-measure equivalents. Dry measure is used primarily for raw fruits and vegetables.

This Measurement		Equals This
2 pints	=	1 quart
4 quarts	=	1 gallon
8 quarts (2 gallons)	=	1 peck
4 pecks	=	1 bushel

What Equals What
(What Weight or Quantity
Equals What Volume)

This Amount		Equals This Measurement
½ ounce Baking Powder	=	4 teaspoons
½ ounce Baking Soda	=	3 teaspoons
1 pound Bananas	=	3 medium
1 pound Ground Beef	=	2 cups
1 ounce Butter	=	2 tablespoons
Butter, size of an egg (2 ounces)	=	4 tablespoons
1 stick Butter (¼ pound)	=	½ cup
½ pound (2 sticks) Butter	=	1 cup
1 pound diced, cooked Chicken	=	3 cups
1 ounce baking Chocolate	=	1 square
1 pound shredded Coconut	=	5 cups
1 pound ground Coffee	=	5⅓ cups
1 pound Cornmeal	=	2½ cups
1 pound Cornstarch	=	3 cups
1 pound Cranberries	=	4 cups
1 pound pitted Dates	=	2 cups
5 whole Eggs	=	1 cup

This Amount		Equals This Measurement
13-14 Egg yolks	=	1 cup
8-12 Egg whites	=	1 cup
1 ounce Fat	=	2 tablespoons
½ pound Fat	=	1 cup
1 pound white Flour	=	4 cups
1 pound whole wheat Flour	=	3½ cups
½ pound candied Fruit or rind	=	1½ cups, chopped
½ pound Lard	=	1 cup
1 Lemon	=	1 tablespoon grated rind
4-6 Lemons	=	1 cup juice
4 ounces Marshmallows	=	16 marshmallows
1 pound quick-cooking Oats	=	5⅓ cups
1 pound chopped Onions	=	3 cups
3-4 medium Potatoes	=	1 pound
1 pound Raisins	=	2⅜ cups
1 pound Rice	=	2 cups
1 pound Tea	=	6½ cups

OVERSIZE WINE BOTTLES

Name		*Capacity*
Magnum	=	about 2/5 gallon
Jeroboam	=	about 4 quarts
Rehoboam	=	about 5 quarts
Methuselah	=	about 6½ quarts
Salmanazar	=	about 12 quarts
Nebuchadnezzar	=	about 20 quarts

SERVINGS & POUNDS

Cereals and Pasta

With the exception of the flaked or puffed cereals, servings given are for the cooked product.

	Size of Serving	Servings per Pound
Cornmeal	¾ cup	16
Flaked corn cereals	1 cup	18 to 24
Other flaked cereals	¾ cup	21
Hominy grits	½ cup	20
Macaroni and noodles	¾ cup	12
Oatmeal	¾ cup	13
Puffed cereals	1 cup	32 to 38
Rice	½ cup	16
Spaghetti	¾ cup	13
Wheat cereals, coarse	¾ cup	12
Wheat cereals, fine	¾ cup	16 to 22

Fruits

Fresh, Dried, Canned, and Frozen

Fresh Fruits	Size of Serving	Servings per Pound as Purchased
Apples	1 medium	3
Apricots	2 medium	5 to 8
Bananas	1 medium	3
Berries, raw	½ cup	4 to 5
Cherries, pitted, cooked	½ cup	2
Oranges	1 medium	3
Peaches	1 medium	4
Pears	1 medium	3
Plums	2 large	4
Rhubarb, cooked	½ cup	4

Dried Fruits	Size of Serving	Servings per Pound as Purchased
Apricots	½ cup, stewed	9
Figs	½ cup, stewed	9
Mixed Fruits	½ cup, stewed	8
Peaches	½ cup, stewed	9
Prunes	½ cup, stewed	8

Canned Fruits	Size of Serving	Servings per Can
8-ounce can	½ cup	2
1-pound can (#303)	½ cup	4
1-pound, 4-ounce can (#2)	½ cup	4 to 5
1-pound, 12-ounce can (#2½)	½ cup	6 to 7
46-ounce can	½ cup	11 to 12

Frozen Fruits or Fruit Juices	*Servings per Package or Can*
10-ounce package	3 to 4
6-ounce can concentrated juice	6

Meat, Poultry, and Fish

The amount of meat, poultry, or fish per serving varies with the amount of bone and fat and the way it is prepared. It also varies with the amount of extenders — such as stuffing, potatoes, or rice — served with the meat.

Meat	*Amount to Buy per Serving*
Much bone or gristle	½ to 1 pound
Medium amounts of bone	⅓ to ½ pound
Little bone	¼ to ⅓ pound
No bone	⅕ to ¼ pound

Poultry, Dressed Weight	*Amount to Buy per Serving*
Chicken, broiling	¼ to ½ bird
Chicken, frying or roasting	¾ to 1 pound
Chicken, stewing	⅓ to ¾ pound
Ducks	1 to 1¼ pounds
Geese	¾ to 1 pound
Turkey	⅔ to ¾ pound

Fish	*Amount to Buy per Serving*
Dressed, large	½ pound
Steaks, fillets	¼ pound
Whole	1 pound

Vegetables

Fresh, Dried, Canned, and Frozen

Fresh Vegetables	Size of Serving	Servings per Pound as Purchased
Asparagus, cut	½ cup	4
Asparagus, spears	4 to 5	4
Beans, lima	½ cup	2 (in pod)
Beans, snap	½ cup	6
Beets, diced	½ cup	4
Broccoli	2 stalks	3 to 4
Brussels sprouts	½ cup	5 to 6
Cabbage, raw shredded	½ cup	7 to 8
Cabbage, cooked	½ cup	4 to 5
Carrots, raw shredded	½ cup	7 to 8
Carrots, cooked	½ cup	5
Cauliflower	½ cup	3
Celery, cooked	½ cup	3 to 4
Collards	½ cup	2
Corn, cut	½ cup	2 (on the cob)
Eggplant	½ cup	4
Onions, cooked	½ cup	4
Parsnips	½ cup	4
Peas	½ cup	2 (in pod)
Potatoes	½ cup	4 to 5
Spinach	½ cup	3 to 4
Sweet potatoes	½ cup	3 to 4
Turnips	½ cup	4

Dried Vegetables	Size of Serving	Servings per Pound as Purchased
Dried beans, cooked	¾ cup	9
Dried peas, lentils, cooked	¾ cup	7

Canned Vegetables	Size of Serving	Servings per Pound as Purchased
8-ounce can	½ cup	2 per can
1-pound can (#303)	½ cup	4 per can
1-pound, 4-ounce can (#2)	½ cup	4 to 5 per can
1-pound, 12-ounce can (#2½)	½ cup	6 to 7 per can
46-ounce can	½ cup	11 to 12 per can

Frozen Vegetables	Size of Serving	Servings per Pound as Purchased
10-ounce package	½ cup	3 to 4 per package

STANDARD SIZES

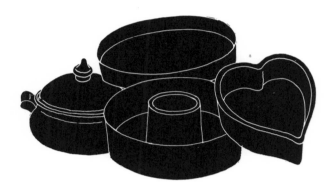

Baking Pans and Sheets

Baking (Cake) Pans	Size
Jelly-Roll	15½ x 10½ x 1 inch
Oblong	10 x 6 x 1½ inches 11 x 7 x 1½ inches 11½ x 7⅜ x 1½ inches 13 x 9½ x 2 inches 13¼ x 8¾ x 1¾ inches
Round	8 x 1½ inches 8⅜ x 1¼ inches 9 x 1½ inches 10 x 1½ inches
Square	8 x 8 x 2 inches 9 x 9 x 1¾ inches 10 x 10 x 1½ inches
Tube	9 x 3½ inches 10 x 4 inches
Baking (Cookie) Sheet	14 x 10 inches 15½ x 12 inches 17 x 14 inches

Casseroles and Roasters

Casseroles	Size if Oblong	Capacity
		10 ounces
	6½ x 7 inches	1 quart
	7 x 10 inches	1½ quarts
	9 x 13 inches	2 quarts
		3 quarts
		3½ quarts

Roasters		Capacity
(Size is designated		7 pounds
by the weight of the		12 pounds
roast the pan will hold.)		18 pounds
		23 pounds

Custard Cups and Tart or Pie Pans

Custard Cups	Size
	5 ounces
	5½ ounces
	6¾ ounces

Tart or Pie Pans	Size
	4¼ inches in diameter, 1⅛ inches deep
	5 inches in diameter, 1 inch deep
	5½ inches in diameter, ¾ inch deep
	6¾ inches in diameter, 1⅛ inches deep
	7½ inches in diameter, 1¼ inches deep
	8 inches in diameter, 1¼ inches deep
	8½ inches in diameter, 1¼ inches deep
	9½ inches in diameter, 1¾ inches deep

Loaf and Muffin (Cupcake) Pans

Loaf Pans	*Size*
	7⅜ x 3⅝ x 2¼ inches
	8 x 4 x 3 inches
	8½ x 4½ x 2½ inches
	9½ x 5¼ x 2¾ inches
	10 x 5 x 3 inches

Muffin (Cupcake) Pans	*Cup Measurement*
Standard pans usually have 6, 8, or 10 cups.	2½ x 1¼ inches
	3 x 1½ inches

SUBSTITUTIONS

If You Don't Have This	*Use This*
1 teaspoon Allspice =	½ teaspoon cinnamon plus ⅛ teaspoon ground cloves
1 teaspoon Baking Powder =	1 teaspoon baking soda plus 1 teaspoon cream of tartar
1 cup canned Beef Bouillon =	1 beef bouillon cube or 1 envelope instant beef broth or 1 teaspoon beef extract dissolved in 1 cup boiling water
1 cup Buttermilk (or sour milk) =	1 cup sweet milk plus 1 tablespoon vinegar
½ cup Catsup, or Chili Sauce =	½ cup tomato sauce plus 2 tablespoons sugar, 1 tablespoon vinegar, ⅛ teaspoon ground cloves
1 square baking Chocolate =	3 tablespoons cocoa powder plus 1 tablespoon shortening
1 cup canned Chicken Broth =	1 chicken bouillon cube or 1 envelope instant chicken broth dissolved in 1 cup boiling water

If You Don't Have This		Use This
¼ cup Cinnamon Sugar	=	¼ cup granulated sugar plus 1 teaspoon cinnamon
1 whole Egg	=	2 egg yolks plus 1 tablespoon water
1 cup presifted Flour	=	1 cup plus 2 tablespoons sifted cake flour
1 tablespoon Cornstarch	=	2 tablespoons flour
1½ cups Corn Syrup	=	1 cup sugar plus ½ cup water
1½ cups diced cooked Ham	=	12-ounce can pork luncheon meat, diced
⅔ cup Honey	=	1 cup sugar plus ⅓ cup water
1 teaspoon Italian Seasoning	=	¼ teaspoon each: oregano, basil, thyme, and rosemary, and a dash of cayenne
½ pound Mushrooms	=	4-ounce can mushroom caps
3-ounce can Chinese Noodles	=	two 2¼-ounce cans potato sticks
1 teaspoon Oregano	=	1 teaspoon marjoram
½ pound ground Pork	=	½ pound sausage meat
1 teaspoon Pumpkin-Pie Spice	=	½ teaspoon cinnamon, ¼ teaspoon ginger, and ⅛ teaspoon each ground nutmeg and cloves
½ cup seedless Raisins	=	½ cup cut prunes
1 pound Shrimp, shelled, deveined, and cooked	=	5-ounce can shrimp
10-ounce package frozen Strawberries	=	1 cup sliced fresh strawberries plus ⅓ cup sugar
Few drops Tabasco Sauce	=	Dash of cayenne or red pepper
½ cup Tartar Sauce	=	6 tablespoons mayonnaise plus 2 tablespoons chopped pickle relish
1 cup canned Tomatoes	=	1⅓ cups chopped fresh tomatoes, simmered for 10 minutes
1 cup Tomato Juice	=	½ cup tomato sauce plus ½ cup water
1 teaspoon Worcestershire Sauce	=	1 teaspoon bottled steak sauce

THIS MAKES THAT

Cereals and Starches

Before Preparation	After Preparation
1 cup cornmeal	4 cups cooked
1 cup macaroni	2 cups cooked
1 cup noodles or spaghetti	2 cups cooked
1 cup quick-cooking oats	1¾ cups cooked
1 cup rice	3 cups cooked
1 medium potato	½ cup mashed potato

Cheese, Cream, and Eggs

Before Preparation	After Preparation
1 pound Cheddar cheese	4 cups shredded
1 cup heavy cream	2 cups whipped
12 hard-boiled eggs	3½ cups chopped

75

Crackers and Bread

Before Preparation	*After Preparation*
1 slice bread	½ cup finely crumbed
18 small crackers	1 cup coarsely crushed
21 small crackers	1 cup finely crushed
9 graham cracker squares	1 cup coarsely crumbed
11 to 12 graham cracker squares	1 cup finely crumbed
1 cup potato chips, firmly packed	½ cup potato chip crumbs
12 thin pretzels	½ cup pretzel crumbs
26 to 30 vanilla wafers	1 cup finely crumbed
9 slices zwieback	1 cup finely crumbed

Fruits

Fresh and Dried

Fresh Fruits

Before Preparation	*After Preparation*
1 pound apples (3 medium)	3 cups pared and diced
1 quart red cherries	2 cups pitted
1 pound cranberries (4¾ cups)	3 to 3½ cups sauce
1 pound Tokay grapes	2¾ cups seeded
1 average lemon	3 to 4 tablespoons juice 1½ teaspoons grated rind
1 average orange	½ cup juice 1 cup diced pulp 1 tablespoon grated rind

Dried Fruits

Before Preparation	After Preparation
1 pound apricots (3 to 3¾ cups)	4½ cups cooked
1 pound unpitted dates (2½ cups)	1¾ cups pitted
1 pound figs (2¼ cups)	4½ cups cooked
1 pound peaches (3⅔ cups)	4½ cups cooked
1 pound pears (2⅔ cups)	5⅓ cups cooked
1 pound prunes (2¾ cups)	4 cups cooked
1 pound raisins (3 to 3¼ cups)	4 cups plumped

Vegetables

Fresh and Dried

Fresh Vegetables

Before Preparation	After Preparation
1 pound beets (4 medium)	2 cups diced
1 pound cabbage	4 cups shredded
1 pound carrots (7 to 8 medium)	4 cups diced
1 pound celery (2 small bunches)	4 cups diced
12 ears corn	3 cups cut kernels
1 pound lima beans in pod	⅔ cup shelled
1 pound peas in pod	1 cup shelled
1 pound potatoes (4 medium)	2½ cups diced

Dried Vegetables

Before Preparation	After Preparation
1 cup lima beans	2½ cups cooked
1 cup red beans	2 cups cooked
1 cup white beans	3 cups cooked

Nuts

Before Preparation	After Preparation
1 pound soft-shell almonds	2 cups shelled
1 pound hard-shell almonds	1 cup shelled
1 pound walnuts in shell	2½ cups shelled
¼ pound walnut meats	1 cup chopped nut meats

KITCHEN TIPS

To **Acidulate** water: Add one table-spoon lemon juice or vinegar to each quart of water.

To thaw frozen **Bread** and rolls, place in a brown paper bag and heat for four to seven minutes in a 325° F. oven. Sprinkle cold water over stale **Breads** and rolls, and warm them in a pre-heated 350° F. oven to freshen them.

Add a few drops of boiling water when creaming sugar and butter to make a smooth-textured **Cake.**

To prevent **Cheese** from becoming hard and dry, wrap in a vinegar-soaked cloth and then seal in plastic wrap before refrigerating.

To melt **Chocolate** easily, place in an oven-proof dish and melt in a slow oven (see Oven Temperatures, p. 53).

Clams will open more readily if first dipped in boiling water.

Sweet pickle juice, used instead of vinegar in a **Coleslaw** dressing, will provide an unusual and delicious taste treat.

A dash of sugar and a little milk added to the cooking water for **Corn-on-the-Cob** greatly enhances the flavor.

When whipping **Cream,** make sure it, bowl, and beaters are cold. Add a dash of salt to cream to make it whip more quickly.

When **Doubling** a recipe, taste the dish before adding double the seasonings.

A tablespoon of salt added to the boiling water will loosen the shells of hard-boiled **Eggs** and make peeling easier.

A pastry cutter or potato masher chops hard-boiled **Eggs** easily and quickly.

When **Egg** Whites are at room temperature, they will beat up faster and lighter.

To double the volume of stiffly beaten **Egg** Whites, add a teaspoon of cold water to them prior to the beating.

To store **Egg** Yolks, cover them with cold water and refrigerate.

Fruit placed in a brown paper bag will ripen quickly.

If **Fruit** is first cored and quartered, it is easier to peel.

Wash and dry **Fruits** and vegetables immediately before using. Refrigerating them while damp will make them soggy.

Cook dried **Fruit** in the same water in which it soaked to enhance the flavor.

Frozen **Fruit** thawed in unopened

packages retains its flavor and color.

To evenly coat foods for **Frying,** shake them in a brown paper bag containing seasoned flour.

For easier unmoulding of **Gelatins,** lightly oil the moulds before filling them.

One tablespoon of milk mixed with a few tablespoons of brown sugar makes a fine **Glaze** for pastries.

A raw potato rubbed over a **Grater** that has been used for cheese will help clean the grater.

If **Gravy** is too thin, try adding beurre manié.

If **Gravy** is too greasy, try adding a small amount of baking soda or an ice cube to which the fat will adhere when the cube is removed.

A pinch of salt added to flour helps keep **Gravy** from becoming lumpy.

To prevent Salad **Greens** from wilting, salt them immediately before serving.

In order to prevent **Icing** from running off a cake, first sprinkle a little flour or cornstarch on top of un-iced cake.

The addition of a lump of butter when cooking fruit for **Jelly** will prevent foam from forming.

A few drops of **Lemon** Juice on sliced bananas, apples, or peaches will prevent them from discoloring.

If whole **Lemons** or **Limes** are rubbed between the hands or rolled on the counter top, they will produce more juice.

Curry powder added to **Mayonnaise** will sharpen the flavor of any salad.

A simple way to tenderize **Meat** is to allow it to sit in a marinade of bottled Italian salad dressing.

To eliminate odor from hands after peeling **Onions,** rinse hands in cool water and rub them with salt.

To extract **Onion** juice: Cut a slice from root end of onion, and scrape juice from center with edge of teaspoon.

An unpeeled, sliced **Orange** added to cooking prunes or applesauce will improve the flavor.

To keep **Parsley** fresh, store it in a tightly closed container in the refrigerator.

To cut **Parsley,** chives, or mint: Wash and dry; mince with sharp knife on a cutting board, or snip with a pair of scissors.

To prevent a **Pie** Crust from becoming soggy during baking, warm the pan for a few minutes before putting in the dough.

To make supple and crisp the skins of baking **Potatoes,** rub them with a little oil or shortening before baking.

When cooking **Rice,** noodles, or spaghetti, a few teaspoons of oil or a pat of butter will prevent the water from boiling over.

In damp climates, the addition of raw rice to the **Salt** Shaker will aid in keeping the salt dry.

To remove excess **Salt** from soup, add a potato and cook it with the soup for about a half hour; then remove it.

If a dish is too sweet, try adding a pinch of **Salt** or a few drops of vinegar.

Use an ice pick to remove the vein from **Shrimp.**

To cut **Sticky** Foods: Use scissors or sharp knife kept wet by dipping frequently in cold water.

To prevent clouding in iced **Tea,** allow brewed tea to come to room temperature before refrigerating.

If brewed **Tea** becomes cloudy, pour a little boiling water in it to clear it.

When brewing one cup of **Tea** or making instant coffee, allow the water to boil two to three minutes to prevent clouding.

Add **Tomatoes** just before serving a salad to ensure their firmness.

The addition of a dash of nutmeg to any **White** Sauce greatly improves the flavor.